Do It Afraid

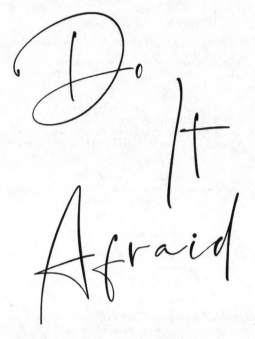

Do It Afraid

EMBRACING COURAGE IN THE FACE OF FEAR

JOYCE MEYER

NEW YORK NASHVILLE

FaithWords
Hachette Book Group
1290 Avenue of the Americas, New York, NY 10104
faithwords.com
twitter.com/faithwords

First Edition: September 2020

FaithWords is a division of Hachette Book Group, Inc. The FaithWords name and logo are trademarks of Hachette Book Group, Inc.

The publisher is not responsible for websites (or their content) that are not owned by the publisher.

The Hachette Speakers Bureau provides a wide range of authors for speaking events. To find out more, go to www.hachettespeakersbureau.com or call (866) 376-6591.

Library of Congress Cataloging-in-Publication Data has been applied for.

ISBNs: 978-1-5460-2630-3 (hardcover), 978-1-5460-1750-9 (large print), 978-1-5460-1761-5 (international), 978-1-5460-2633-4 (ebook), 978-1-5460-1564-2 (signed edition), 978-1-5460-1563-5 (BN.com signed edition)

Printed in the United States of America

LSC-C

10 9 8 7 6 5 4 3 2 1

CONTENTS

Fear is everywhere, and it affects everyone. It has been around since the beginning of time, and it will be here as long as the earth remains. Fear rules many people, but it doesn't have to be that way. Fear is said to be *False Evidence Appearing Real*, and that is an accurate definition because fear is rooted in lies the devil tells us. When we believe them, fear takes root in our hearts and minds.

Although fear will never totally disappear from our lives, we can confront it and overcome it. Courage is not the absence of fear; it is moving forward in the presence of fear. Courageous people do what they believe in their hearts they should do, no matter how they feel or what kinds of doubts and fearful thoughts fill their minds.

If we were to take time to notice how often our reactions to people and circumstances are rooted in fear, we would be amazed. We would also learn a great deal about ourselves. People can and often do spend their entire lives reacting to situations in ways that prevent them from being the people they truly want to be, never realizing that their lives feel empty because they have allowed fear to dictate their decisions.

If you are in a room enjoying conversation with a few friends when suddenly someone joins the group and you immediately feel intimidated, the culprit is fear. That fear may be unreasonable because you may not even know the person, and there would be no reason for them to provoke fear in you. When something like this happens, your fearful reaction may be related to a specific personality type that reminds you of someone who hurt you earlier in your life. Or perhaps the person who intimidates you is better looking or better educated than you are, and that makes you feel insecure. Or there may be no reason at all for you to be afraid except that the devil wants to torment you. You could feel intimidated for numerous reasons, none of which are related to the other person at all.

In such a circumstance, the wise course of action is to ask God why you reacted the way you did and then watch and wait for Him to speak to your heart. The answer may come immediately, or it may take a while, but if you seek to understand yourself, you will find truth, and the truth will make you free (John 8:32).

Let me urge you not to allow fear to push you around and simply put up with it. Neither should you go through your life blaming other people for your misery. Take ownership of your problems and open your heart to God, and He will help bring light into darkness (situations you don't understand). If you can understand fear and how it operates, you can be free from it.

The first part of this book will help you understand fear and recognize how it works in your life. The second part will help you confront fear. In the third part, you will learn about mindsets that will position you for freedom from some of the most common fears people face. I pray that as you read and study this book you will experience freedom from fear, which is something Jesus died to give you.

While fear is understandable under certain circumstances—earthquakes, hurricanes, fires, viruses, and other situations—being afraid does not change the experiences the enemy uses to make us afraid. Fear will never make circumstances better, but it will rob us of our strength to deal with them and of our ability to think clearly in the midst of them. The apostle John wrote, "Fear hath torment" (1 John 4:18 KJV), and even when feeling afraid is understandable, it does nothing but torment us.

Fear is the devil's favorite tool in the toolbox of schemes he uses to steal, kill, and destroy God's good plan for us (John 10:10). He uses it to prevent our progress in every area of our lives. He uses it to hold us back, to get us to run away from things we should confront, and simply to cause us emotional suffering. People allow fear to control them to varying degrees, but we can decide not to let it control us at all in any area for "God gave us a spirit not of fear but of power and love and self-control" (2 Tim. 1:7 ESV).

PART 1

Understanding Fear

Basically there are two paths you can walk: faith or fear. It's impossible to simultaneously trust God and not trust God.

Charles Stanley

Choosing God's Word over the Stronghold of Fear

During my early childhood, I had a speech impediment that made me feel pretty insecure. One day, my third-grade teacher made me walk to the front of the classroom and then ridiculed me in front of my classmates. That was decades ago, but Satan still uses that memory to trigger anxiety attacks in my mind.

On any given day, *whatever I am doing becomes difficult* if I'm struggling with anxiety. So, I really appreciate Joyce's teachings in *Do It Afraid.*

Two scriptures I've come to depend on are Philippians 4:6, "Do not be anxious about anything, but in everything by prayer and supplication with thanksgiving let your requests be made known to God" (ESV), and Philippians 4:13, "I can do all things through him who strengthens me" (ESV).

Recently, my boss asked me to speak candidly (in front of my peers) about the challenges we are facing in the midst of a major systems overhaul in the office. For me, it would have been easier to bow out gracefully and keep my thoughts to myself. But I knew that God wanted me to follow through. It's like He was saying, "If you'll just be open and honest about your frustrations, then I will open doors that will lead to positive changes."

I went through with it. *I did it afraid.* And the responses I received were positive. But later that night, I was so anxious that I couldn't get to sleep! Attacks from the enemy were coming left and right: *What if my feedback wasn't valuable? What if I'm just causing more problems at work?* What I needed to do was agree with God's Word and start speaking it out loud to drown out all that negative noise:

I will not be anxious, because God hears my prayers (Phil. 4:6).

I can do anything I have to do through Christ, who gives me strength (Phil. 4:13).

God is for me and not against me (Rom. 8:31).

Greater is He who is in me than he who is in the world (1 John 4:4).

God's Word is life for me. It keeps me going forward when, on the inside, I feel like retreating.

—LaVondria

CHAPTER 1

It's Time to Make a Choice

This day I call the heavens and the earth as witnesses against you that I have set before you life and death, blessings and curses. Now choose life, so that you and your children may live.

Deuteronomy 30:19

God has a good plan for our lives, but the devil also has a plan, and it is *not* a good one. The apostle John explained this simply, saying, "The thief comes only to steal and kill and destroy; I have come that they may have life, and have it to the full" (John 10:10). God's plan is received through placing our faith in what He has said to us in His Word, and the devil's plan is received through believing his lies. The devil is a liar; he is the father of lies and the truth is not in him (John 8:44).

God has given us free will, which means we can do what we want to do. We have choices, and each one we make brings a result. God said in Deuteronomy 30:19 that He gives us two choices: life or death, blessing or curse. Then He even told us which one to choose. He said to choose life, "so that you and your children may live." Even though He told us which one to choose, He still requires us to make the choice. God's good plan for our lives won't just automatically happen and neither will the devil's evil plan. We must choose one or the other.

You might think, *Surely nobody would intentionally choose the devil's evil plan for their life.* But people do choose his plan through a lack of knowledge regarding him and his evil ways. The prophet Hosea said that God's people are destroyed for a lack of knowledge (Hosea 4:6). My purpose in writing this book is to help you gain knowledge about fear, how fear works in your life, and how to break free from it so you cannot be deceived.

We make one big choice when we decide to receive Jesus as Savior and Lord; then we spend our lives making daily choices that line up with God's Word. When we are in a tense situation at work, we can choose to tell the truth instead of a lie. When a clerk doesn't charge us enough for a certain purchase, it is up to us to do the right thing and make them aware that we owe more money instead of keeping quiet and considering ourselves lucky.

If I were to ask you to guess who tempts you to lie or keep quiet about a work situation, I'm pretty sure you would know the answer. Likewise, if I asked who suggested that you tell the truth and speak up about owing more money, I am sure you know the correct answer to that also. But in both cases you would have to choose what you would do. If you make right choices according to God's will, you experience blessing. But if you choose what you know is wrong, you will face consequences you won't like or enjoy.

Living the Good Life

The apostle Paul wrote:

> For we are God's [own] handiwork (His workmanship), recreated in Christ Jesus, [born anew] that we may do

those good works which God predestined (planned beforehand) for us [taking paths which He prepared ahead of time], that we should walk in them [living the good life which He prearranged and made ready for us to live].

Ephesians 2:10 AMPC

We might read these words and think, *Everybody will choose the good life*, but sadly, there are more who don't choose it than those who do. Why? Because the devil lies to them and makes them think they can make wrong choices and still have right results. He convinces them that they will be the lucky ones who won't experience problems because of bad choices.

The Bible says that our sin always finds us out and that the result of sin is death (Num. 32:23; Rom. 6:23). This "death" is not always the cessation of life. More often, it is the loss of peace, joy, and a life worth living. We can always repent of our sin, receive God's complete forgiveness, and go on to live good lives, but there are times we may still have to bear the consequences of our wrong actions. A person may commit murder and God will forgive him if he truly repents. His family and even the family of the person he killed may forgive him, but he will still have to go to prison. It is important for us to realize that our actions carry consequences.

Notice also that Ephesians 2:10 tells us that God arranges a good life for us, but we must walk in it. We have to choose God's ways. He is always drawing us toward His will, and His grace is always present to enable us to do the right thing, but once again let me be clear that God won't force us to do what is right. We are partners with God in our lives. We *cannot* do His part, and He *will not* do our part. He sets before us life and death, good and evil. The choice is ours.

Whether we walk in faith or fear is a decision we must make many times throughout our lives. I don't think it would be a stretch to say we may need to make that choice daily.

> Whether we walk in faith or fear is a decision we must make many times throughout our lives.

My father was an abusive man who controlled his family through fear. It was actually the devil working through him, but he made choices about how he would live, and he had to bear the consequences of those choices in his life. Although he repented and received Jesus at the age of eighty-three, he lived a miserable life for eighty-three years and died when he was eighty-six. I'm glad to know he is in heaven, but what he did had a lasting impact on a lot of people. It is good for us to remember that our choices affect the people around us as well as our own lives.

My mother was ruled by fear, and because of her refusal to confront her fear, both my brother and I suffered. My father sexually abused me, and my mother knew he was doing it, but fear was so strong in her life that she ignored the truth and eventually had mental problems as a result of the deeply rooted guilt and shame she felt.

When my mother was in her seventies, she apologized to me for what she let my father do. She explained to me that she simply could not face the scandal and was afraid she couldn't take care of my brother and me by herself. As you can see, her decisions were based on fear, and all of us suffered because of that, including her.

If you are allowing fear to rule your decisions, you are missing the good life God has planned for you, and there is a strong possibility that your fear is adversely affecting other people in your life, too. It is time to make the choice to let God help you break free from fear.

Although you may have been ruled by fear in the past, you can choose today to confront fear and become the courageous person God wants you to be. It is not too late. It is never too late to do the right thing.

> It is never too late to do the right thing.

Choose Faith

I have heard that when fear knocks on our door, we should send faith to answer. We can conquer fear, but only with faith. When the devil tells us, "You can't," we should remember that God tells us, "You can." Even though we may feel fear, we can move forward in faith.

When Peter saw Jesus walking on water and wanted to do the same, he got out of the boat and began taking steps. As long as he kept his eyes on Jesus, he did indeed walk on water, but when he began to look at the storm and the raging waves around him, he grew frightened and started to sink. Jesus reached out and saved him, but He also lovingly rebuked him for his fear, asking him why he had such little faith and so much doubt (Matt. 14:25–31).

God never stops loving us and doesn't even become angry with us because we choose fear, but it does make Him sad because He wants us to live the best life we can live. He sent Jesus so we could have life and have it abundantly (John 10:10).

God Prepares Us for What He Has Planned for Us

After God called me to teach His Word, I needed a lot of time to study. In that season of my life, I had a husband and three children and certainly couldn't leave all my responsibilities and go to

Bible college. I also had a full-time job. So I studied as much as I could, but I simply did not have enough time to study as much as I needed to. I was teaching a small Bible study group each Tuesday evening at our home, but God had bigger plans, and I needed time to prepare for what He had planned for me.

I sensed very strongly that God wanted me to quit my job so I could have time at home to study several hours every day, but there was a problem. Had I quit my job, we wouldn't have had enough money to pay our monthly bills, and we definitely would not have had money for emergencies or extra things.

I finally tried to bargain with God: I quit my full-time job and took a part-time job. After only a short time, I got fired. I had always been a good employee—certainly not the type to be fired—but the office manager disliked me from the moment I took the job, and no matter what I did, it wasn't right. When I was fired, it was evident to me that God told me to "quit" my job, not to get a part-time job.

Partial obedience is not faith. It is a little faith mixed with a lot of fear and self-reliance, and it doesn't work. I was afraid we wouldn't have enough without my income, so even though I wanted to be obedient to God, I wanted a backup plan just in case we didn't get the miracle we needed each month.

This same scenario is not uncommon and many people try to do what I did—only under different circumstances. In 1 Samuel 13 and 15 we see two instances when King Saul tried partial obedience and ended up losing his kingdom because of it. Each time he offered excuses that sounded good, but God expects us to obey Him, not offer excuses for why we didn't obey Him.

> God expects us to obey Him, not offer excuses for why we didn't obey Him.

One instance of Saul's disobedience was due to fear (1 Samuel 13:1–14), and the other was the result of greed (1 Samuel 15:1–23). Let's be very careful not to make excuses for our disobedience. An excuse may sound plausible to us, but God will not accept it.

If you send your teenagers to the store to get milk and they come back with orange juice, they have disobeyed you. They may reason that orange juice is still something to drink and might even offer you the excuse that they got it because it was on sale. But the point is that they did not do what you asked them to do.

When God is preparing us for something big that He wants us to do, He allows us to go through many tests of obedience. Some may seem insignificant to us, but they are as important as anything we might consider big. If we cannot be trusted in little things, we will never be made ruler over bigger things (Matt. 25:21, 23).

After losing my part-time job, I did what God asked me to do and quit working outside the home altogether. I was very fearful concerning finances because each month we needed a miracle to pay our bills in full and have provision for anything extra that came up. Each month, we were around forty dollars short of having enough to pay the bills, but learning how to trust God for that small amount helped prepare us to trust God for the large amounts we need now to support the work He allows us to do around the world. I will never forget how amazing it was to watch God provide for us each month. He did it in a variety of ways and never left us without what we needed.

When I quit my job, I made the right choice, but had I made a wrong choice, my life would be very different than how it is now. What kind of choices are you making in your life right now? Are they choices to obey God, to choose life and blessing? Are they choices you will be happy with later on? I pray you are making right choices and that if you haven't been in the past, today will be a new beginning for you. Choose faith, not fear. It is never too late for a new beginning with God.

When you are afraid, do the thing you are afraid of and soon you will lose your fear of it.

Norman Vincent Peale

Doing It Afraid at Sixty Years Old

Never in my nearly sixty years did I think I would ever learn to swim. I didn't really think it mattered anymore. When I was young, maybe. But I wasn't a child any longer. I didn't plan to swim the English Channel or compete in the Olympics, so why would I want to learn to swim? And why, then, was I getting the nagging impression that I needed to learn?

Now, I know swimming is not a problem for many people. It's great exercise. It's exhilarating, they say. And it's fun. But for me, it was terrifying! And at the time, I thought it always would be. Water was my phobia.

When I reflect on how my fear of water started, I immediately remember the tragic drowning of my childhood friend. I can still hear his mother's scream piercing through our open windows that summer night. Even now, it saddens my heart to think how water took my friend from me. Then a few years later, my sister's classmate drowned during a swimming class at school. I'll never forget the broken expression on her coach's face at the wake. Indescribable. I could only conclude that water was bad and, other than for a bath, there would never be a reason for me to be in it.

But it slowly began to dawn on me that God was speaking. It was time to confront more than just my fear of swimming and face fear itself! I instinctively knew that this issue was bigger than I thought. Fear had stifled too much of my life. One day I shared what was on my heart with some coworkers, and then I knew I had to follow through. So, I joined the YMCA and signed up for beginners' classes.

It was just as I suspected. God was up to something in my life. As I timidly progressed through each lesson—and did it afraid—I experienced His presence and peace in a profound way. As I was learning to swim, I was also learning to trust on a whole new level.

Swimming is a lifetime achievement for me, literally. Not only is it great exercise, it is really exhilarating. And more than anything, it's fun. But the most outstanding accomplishment for me has been learning to trust God on a more personal level, in the deep, so to speak. Knowing He is with me in every situation I face, I don't dread what's ahead, because whatever comes, I know He will guide me through it. After all, God set me free from the fear and helped me learn to swim. It is never too late to do it afraid.

—Carolyn

CHAPTER 2

Do It Afraid

*Have I not commanded you? Be strong and courageous. Do
not be afraid; do not be discouraged, for the Lord your God
will be with you wherever you go.*

Joshua 1:9

God had a big job for Joshua to do, and before sending him out
to do it, He told him not to be afraid. We need to understand
the meaning of the word *fear* in order to rightly understand what
God was saying to Joshua.

Over the years I have studied a lot about fear and made several
interesting observations about what it means. One of the most
powerful descriptions of fear that I have encountered is "to take
flight," or "to run from." We can also describe fear as an unpleasant emotion caused by the belief (thought) of harm or pain. A
full definition of fear involves more than these ideas, but I want
us to focus on the fact that to fear is to run away from something
due to an unpleasant emotion or feeling that we may suffer or be
harmed.

If we look at fear as running away from something, I think we
can see that God wasn't telling Joshua not to *feel* fear. Instead,
He was warning him that he would feel fear, and that when he
did he was not to flee because He (God) would be with him.

Like many people, I spent years trying to get rid of the feeling of fear. I never saw it for what it was—a feeling or an emotion based on wrong thinking. When I looked at my problems or potential problems, I saw them without seeing God.

Throughout Scripture, God said in several different ways, "Fear not, for I am with you." He said it to Joshua and to many others (Deut. 31:6; Isa. 41:10; Isa. 43:1; Mark 6:50; Rev. 1:17). As a matter of fact, the only reason I can find in God's Word for us not to fear is simply that God is with us. No matter what is happening in our lives, God is greater, and He is with us. We may not know what He will do to help us or when He will do it, but knowing He is with us should be enough. He is for us, not against us, and if God is for us, it does not matter who is against us (Rom. 8:31), for God is greater than anyone or anything else (1 John 4:4).

I mistakenly thought that as long as I felt fear, I could not do what I wanted to do or felt I should do. I was wasting my life waiting for fear to go away. I prayed diligently for God to take away the fear, but my prayer never got answered because I was praying for the wrong thing. I should have been praying for God to give me the courage to go forward in the presence of fear and not let it stop me.

> I was wasting my life waiting for fear to go away.

Understanding that we can feel fear and move forward anyway has been life-changing for me and many other people. It came through a story I read about a woman who had been imprisoned by fear for most of her life. She wouldn't drive or go out after dark, and she lived an isolated, lonely life. Basically, she didn't do anything she wanted to do because she was afraid. As she was telling her woes to a Christian friend, the friend looked at her and simply said, "Why don't you just do it afraid?"

When I read that, I felt as though I had been living in the dark for years and suddenly the lights turned on. I saw it! I didn't need to wait for feelings of fear to go away because they probably never would, but I could do what I wanted to do, or felt God wanted me to do, even if I did it while feeling afraid.

Fear has no real power over us if we understand what it truly is. It has no power to harm us because it only shows us images and causes us to think about what harmful things may happen to us if we go forward.

I know a woman who was afraid to fly in an airplane. Her husband traveled a great deal for his job, and their children were grown and away from home, so he wanted her to go with him. She wanted to go but thought she couldn't because she was afraid. After many years of staying home alone while he traveled around the world, she decided to do it afraid. The first few times were very hard; she said she felt shaky and as if she couldn't breathe. But she was determined. Now she flies often and has no problem at all.

You see, as long as Satan can stop you with fear, he will. But if you confront it, eventually even the feelings of fear will go away— at least they will go away in the area in which you confront them. You will need to confront new areas of fear as they come up throughout your life, but never forget that the only way to live free from fear is to confront it, or "do it afraid."

> The only way to live free from fear is to confront it, or "do it afraid."

I am not suggesting that you do foolish things simply to prove you're not afraid. I am not a very good swimmer, so I am not going to jump off of a cliff into water that is fifty feet deep. Some fears are based on real facts and those fears can actually protect us from harm. We know that fire burns, so we don't stick our hands into flames. We don't walk out into the middle of a highway with traffic coming at us both ways. I am not talking about those kinds of situations, but I am saying that anything God asks you to do, you can do it even if you have to do it afraid, knowing that He is always with you. Even things that you simply want to do, as long as they are within the guidelines of God's will found in His Word, you should be able to do without allowing fear to stop you.

Little Fears and Big Fears

Sometimes all it takes to be courageous is simply to keep trying day after day. Courage is not giving up no matter how long it takes to secure victory. I can't promise you that if you confront fear it will go away in a day, or even in a thousand days, because it always shows up somewhere. But remember that freedom from fear doesn't mean the absence of its existence, but the refusal to let it control your decisions and actions.

Fear does not always show up just for the big events in your life. It is lurking somewhere all the time, hoping for a chance to jump on board in your life, even if it only causes a vague feeling of dread or doubt. Maybe you want to have a baby but are afraid you won't be a good parent, so you keep putting it off. Maybe you want to change your hair color, but you're afraid you won't like it, so you just settle for keeping your hair the way it is. Whether the fear you experience concerns something you would consider big or something small, all fear should be resisted. The more you let it hang around in your life the more comfortable it will become and, sadly, the more comfortable you may become with it. Sometimes we grow so accustomed to something that we forget that it is not the way things should be. Don't let fear stay so long that it begins to seem normal or acceptable in your life.

We Don't Have to Live in Fear

I grew up in an atmosphere of total fear, so for me fear was a normal state in which to live. I didn't even know there was another way to live until God began teaching me how to live the good life He had prearranged for me. I lived with a vague sense of dread most of the time. It wasn't attached to anything in particular; it was simply there, and I couldn't remember a time when it wasn't.

One day when I was putting on my makeup I became aware of an ominous feeling around me. I asked the Lord, "What is this feeling I have around me all the time?" And, I might say, to my surprise, He answered me. Immediately in my spirit I heard the words "evil forebodings."

An evil foreboding is a fearful or threatening feeling that something bad is going to happen at any moment. The Bible says, "All the days of the desponding and afflicted are made evil [by anxious thoughts and forebodings]" (Prov. 15:15 AMPC).

When God spoke to my heart, I knew what my problem was and why those evil forebodings had easy access to me. All of my life I had one bad thing after another happen to me. I was abused by my father, abandoned by my mother, not allowed to have friends or participate in any after school activities, and other disappointing, unfair situations. I became so accustomed to being disappointed that I was actually afraid to expect anything good, so instead I just waited quietly for whatever the next painful or disappointing circumstance might be.

When we are born again, the Bible says we are born into a living hope (1 Peter 1:3). No matter how bad our situation may be, in Jesus there is always hope for positive change. He wants us to expect good things, not bad ones. We do not have to live in fear!

Don't Just Put Up with It

Too often we become accustomed to something and just put up with it when we should be confronting it and moving past it. If you have allowed someone to bully, manipulate, or control you, don't just cower under that behavior and put up with it—confront the person intimidating you.

That person will probably become angry, but the longer you let their bad behavior go on, the worse it will become. You say, "I'm afraid," and I say, "Do it afraid," because God is with you. Pray and ask God to help you and guide you before you take action and then, when you sense the time is right, go with God and get it over with.

Which seems worse to you: confronting your fears or putting up with them all your life? Fear, like most bullies, will back down when confronted.

> Fear, like most bullies, will back down when confronted.

For many years I put up with a nagging pain in my back, and finally one day I could barely walk to go get the help I needed. Fear can be the same way. We put up with it like a little nagging irritation until one day we realize we have wasted a great deal of our time and have not enjoyed much of our lives.

That was my mother's story. She gave in to fear when she was in her early twenties and missed having a good life. She died at the age of ninety and I doubt that she ever had one full day when she didn't regret the decisions she had made. She lived in a tiny world that mainly consisted of trying to keep my father happy, because his anger was not easy to deal with. He died before she did, so she had a few years of peace before her time on earth was up, and I'm glad she did. She barely left her room at the assisted living facility where she spent her last few years and said she stayed there because she liked the peace and quiet. That was something she had never had, but it was there for her all along—she simply had to make the decision to not put up with the abuse anymore.

Help is available, but we must choose to receive it. Ephesians 6 talks about spiritual warfare. It instructs us to lift up the shield of faith and with it quench all the flaming darts of the evil one (Eph. 6:16). Fear is a flaming dart that comes straight from the enemy. The fact that we *feel* fear does not mean we have to *live* in fear, allowing it to dictate what we will and won't do. We can choose to face fear with faith. We can feel fear and still do it afraid!

You can conquer almost any fear if you will only make up your mind to do so. For remember, fear doesn't exist anywhere except in the mind.

Dale Carnegie

Defeating Fear by Focusing on Right Thoughts

I have a theory that fears have wings. You see, I have a fear of birds—a purely unjustified, irrational fear of their pointy beaks and sharp talons.

My father also has this fear, but his is based on a real-life, personal experience. When he was very young, he was attacked by a rooster and actually spent time in the hospital as a result of his injuries. As he grew, he carried the fear that birds are dangerous. He viewed them as definitely not to be trusted and avoided them whenever possible.

When I came along, as good fathers do, he protected me. He would keep birds away from me and me away from them. After all, just look at those beady little eyes.

My father is a brave, wonderful man who taught me to not be afraid of much of anything. He would never purposefully pass along fear—but fears have wings. Without realizing it, our experiences and actions teach our children, and fears fly from one person to the next. So birds and I were not friends.

I travel a lot and am thankfully not bothered by fear's usual suspects, like spiders or snakes, but put a bird in the mix and the story is slightly different. Unreasonable, yes, but I have learned to manage those initial feelings with God's help and by focusing on the right thoughts rather than the wrong ones. I know that the probability of a bird hurting me is not high, and while I still dislike the winged critters, I'm not greatly impacted by them because I have decided that I will not let fear control me.

I have also purposed not to let my fear take wing and land on my children. They and birds get along just fine, in spite of the fact that I prefer not to go in the aviary at the zoo with them. I'm not really afraid, but I don't have to hang out with birds just for fun, either.

—Ginger

CHAPTER 3

I Will Not Fear

The Lord is with me; I will not be afraid.

Psalm 118:6

When the psalmist David wrote, "I will not be afraid," I don't think he meant that he would not *feel* fear. I think he was declaring that when he did feel afraid, he would not let fear control him. Each of us should have that same attitude. In fact, it is the only acceptable attitude for a Christian to have. Fear is not from God, and we should resist it firmly in the power of the Holy Spirit. To resist it means to choose not to let it affect our decisions.

"I am with you always" is a promise from God (Matt. 28:20). Actually, it is one of the most important promises in God's Word. He promises to forgive us when we sin, and that is wonderful, but equally wonderful is His promise to be with us. There is no place you have ever been that God was not there and no place you will ever be that He will not be there also. He is omnipresent, which means He is everywhere all the time. He sees everything, knows everything, and has all power. The really good news is that He is our Father, and we are His children. God wants us to believe that we don't have to be afraid of anything because He is with us. He is good, and He will take care of us as His children.

I suggest that you spend more time asking God to draw you closer to Him and reveal His presence to you than you do asking

Him to fix your problems. God wants to help us with our troubles, but even more than that He

> "Seek God's presence, not
> His presents."

wants us to want Him. I say it this
way: "Seek God's presence, not His
presents."

The same promise of God's presence that David had was also
made to Noah (Gen. 6:18), Abraham and Sarah (Gen. 17:7, 19;
Rom. 4:17), Jacob (Gen. 28:15), Joseph and Mary (Matt. 1:23), and
Paul (Acts 18:10).These servants of God had no need to be fearful
because He had promised to be with them wherever they went.
That promise kept them strong through dark and painful times.
David said, "Even though I walk through the darkest valley, I will
fear no evil, for you are with me" (Ps. 23:4).

The promise of God's presence, which He made to people in
biblical times, is your promise, too. God never promises that we
won't endure difficulties, but He does promise to be with us in
them. Jesus is called Immanuel, which means "God with us"
(Matt. 1:23). Because of that we know that eventually our problems will come to an end and we will come out stronger than we
were before we went through them.

We can learn to perceive God's presence without actually feeling Him physically. The devil can take advantage of our emotions
and deceive us if we depend too much on the way we feel or don't
feel. God wants us to believe like little children, who seem to
have spiritual perception that some adults lack. This is because
they are willing to believe what seems to be impossible.

I heard about a little girl who was asked how she knew that
Jesus lived in her heart. She answered, "Because when I put my
hand on my heart I can feel Him walking around in there." The
beating of our hearts is proof of the presence of God.

One of the most thrilling aspects of my relationship with God is when I recognize His presence. It is often in small things, but they are things that mean a lot to me. When my children call me regularly to tell me they love me, I know it is God loving me through them. When my husband hugs me every morning and says, "How's my baby?" I know it is God giving me a hug. When I am in a restaurant and the manager comes and moves me to my favorite table, I know it is a "wink" from God. We are often so focused on looking for a huge miracle in our lives that we miss the hundreds of small miracles that happen around us all the time.

Develop a habit of looking for God everywhere, and you might be surprised where He will show up. Be "God is with me" minded. God says that if you seek Him, you will find him (Jer. 29:13).

> Develop a habit of looking for God everywhere, and you might be surprised where He will show up.

Jacob was a scheming trickster who stole his brother Esau's birthright through lies and deception (Gen. 27:1–40). He then spent the next twenty years running and hiding from Esau, in fear that he would kill him. Jacob was certainly not a spiritual giant with impeccable morals, yet God gave him a dream in which he saw a ladder extending from the earth upward to heaven. On that ladder, the angels of God were ascending and descending (Gen. 28:10–22). One might initially think the ladder was for Jacob to try to climb up to God, but it was actually for God to come down to him. God meets us where we are, and Jacob was in great need of help.

When Jacob awoke, he realized the dream was from God and said, "Surely the Lord is in this place, and I was not aware of it" (Gen. 28:16). An ordinary, nowhere place became a special place where God was. One of our great tragedies in life is that God is

with us and we are often not aware of it. Our faith would soar
to new heights if we would learn
to recognize God's presence in the
ordinary aspects of daily life.

> One of our great tragedies in
> life is that God is with us and
> we are often not aware of it.

You don't need to go to a church
with stained-glass windows and
an altar with a cross to find God, because He is with you right
now. He is with you while you are in the grocery store, driving
in traffic, paying your bills, sitting at your desk at work, or playing ball with your children. God doesn't want us to merely visit
Him for an hour on Sunday morning. When we realize that God
is with us, then and only then will we be delivered from fear. It
will still lurk around us trying to gain entrance into our lives,
we will still hear fear in our thoughts and feel it in our emotions,
but we will "do it afraid," because we are confident that He is
with us.

Distractions

Fear creeps in when we forget that God is with us and begin striv-
ing and struggling to do things in our human strength. Remember that God said over and over to many of His servants, "Fear
not, for I am with you." Fear can be and often is very subtle. It
may appear in the form of worry, dread, or even jealousy.

Let me explain. Let's suppose that a middle-aged woman has
never been married and her deep desire is to meet the right man
and be his wife. While she waits, many of her friends get married. She attends their weddings and pretends to be happy for
them, but secretly she is jealous and envious. I think that her fear
of never getting married herself is the root cause of her jealousy.

We are not jealous of what anyone else has if we have the same thing. Fear comes when we are afraid we will be left out or have to do without what we want.

As a matter of fact, the fear of not getting what we want is the cause of many of our problems. It causes worry, anxiety, and the development of endless plans that never work. Proverbs 16:9 says that our minds may plan our way, but God directs our steps. It is no wonder that so many of *our* plans don't work the way we desire them to. God's thoughts and ways are higher than ours (Isa. 55:8–9). He loves us, so when we try to force a plan that He knows won't be good for us, He lovingly interferes and blocks its success because He has something much better in His plan.

Jesus said that when the seed of God's Word is sown in our hearts, distractions and the cares of this world come and steal that seed (Mark 4:14–19 AMPC). Satan is afraid that we will grow spiritually if we stay focused and let the Word take root in our hearts, so he finds endless ways to distract us from Jesus and His Word. Just think about that for a minute. What kinds of useless things steal your time with the Lord and distract you from God's presence? How often are you praying when a distraction or an interruption comes and derails you from your purpose? Learning to stay focused is possibly one of life's biggest challenges, especially in today's culture, where multitasking, staying busy, and working hard are applauded and celebrated.

Let's look at the story of Mary and Martha as an example of what Jesus said about distractions. Martha invited Jesus to come to her home, and I am sure she was eager to hear what He had to say, but she became distracted with all the preparations to host Him. It sounds like she was cooking, cleaning, and making sure everything was just right during His visit, but her sister Mary simply sat at Jesus' feet. That was amazing. In that day, when someone sat at a rabbi's feet, it meant that person desired to be his disciple. No other rabbi in history had ever had a woman as his disciple, but Jesus did.

Ultimately Martha became so frustrated because she was doing all the work while Mary was sitting and listening to Jesus that she complained to Jesus about the situation. Jesus replied to her that she was anxious and worried about many things, but Mary had chosen the one thing that was more important than any other (Luke 10:38–42).

Was Jesus implying that Martha should not work? No, His implication was that she could be with Him while she worked, or even better she could delay the work for a while and take advantage of something more important at the moment than cleaning and cooking. Martha had invited Jesus into her home but was missing out on His presence because of worry. She had good intentions but got distracted, as many of us do.

This story is not teaching us not to *work*; it is teaching us not to *worry* and not to allow the distractions of daily life to cause us to miss the presence of God. We can do our work with Jesus instead of letting it take us away from Him. We may not be able to have Him on our mind every single moment of the day, but we can stop occasionally to simply recognize

> We can do our work with Jesus instead of letting it take us away from Him.

that He is with us and perhaps say, "Thank You, Lord, that You never leave me."

We can remember to stop and thank God for all the prayers He has answered and the amazing things He has done for us.

Yesterday Dave and I and our daughter were going to see an Elvis Presley impersonator (yes, I like Elvis), and our daughter's seat was not with us. She and I prayed and asked the Lord to have a seat next to us become available so she could sit with us. The people in the box office had already told me that the entire theater was sold out, so I was praying for the impossible. It turned out that four seats next to our daughter were open, and we were able to sit together. Coincidence? I don't think so!

That evening I asked my daughter if she realized God had answered our prayer, and she said, "Oh, that's right, we prayed for empty seats." So often we are like the nine lepers who were healed but failed to go back to Jesus and say thank you (Luke 17:11–19). We are excited about what God has done for us, but Satan wants to distract us so we will not remember to say, "Father, thank You for answering my prayer."

A good way to be more aware of God's presence is to take five minutes each day and mentally review all the activities of the previous day and see if you can find places where God definitely showed up, but you were too busy to notice. This morning as I did that, I remembered again the situation at the theater and marveled at God's goodness to care about something as minor as our theater seats.

God wants to be involved in our entire lives and in everything we do. That's what it means to walk with God. He doesn't want just a short visit on Sunday morning when we go to church; He wants to do life with us. He wants us to abide in Him, which means to live, to dwell and remain in and with Him at all times. Apart from Him we can do nothing.

> God doesn't want just a short visit on Sunday morning when we go to church; He wants to do life with us.

I am the vine; you are the branches. If you remain in me
and I in you, you will bear much fruit; apart from me you
can do nothing.

John 15:5

God is never more than a thought away. Think about Him and
talk to Him throughout the day. Recognizing His presence will
give you courage and confidence rather than fear.

Fear defeats more people than any other one thing in the world.

Ralph Waldo Emerson

Speak Faith Instead of Fear!

I still remember in detail a moment in the doctor's office when I was eight years old. My little sister sat on the examination table while I waited quietly in a wooden chair nearby.

She was there for a vaccination, and as the nurse barreled into the room and grabbed the needle, she joked, "Think we should give this to your sister?" "Yeah!" my sister joked right back. The room filled with laughter as the nurse and my mom tried to lighten the mood.

But it wasn't funny to me. *Is she really going to give me the shot?* I wondered.

I could smell the rubbing alcohol and sense the sterility of the room. And slowly, I slid out of the chair and onto the floor—I had turned white as a ghost, I'm told, and passed right out.

I woke up to that nurse saying, "I guess your sister just doesn't like needles!"

No, she really doesn't like needles, I said to myself.

For some reason, those words became rooted deep inside of me. From that point on, in any appointment where I *might* need a shot, I'd start with the statement: "Uh, I just *really* don't like needles."

When I had to get my blood drawn, the phlebotomist tried to take my mind off of what was happening by asking me questions. I passed out three times that day!

After a dentist appointment nine years ago, I heard the most frightening-to-me words: *You have a small cavity.* I lost countless nights of sleep being gripped by fear of the needle that would be used when it had to be filled.

Those moments and a number of others reinforced my confession: "I just really don't like needles."

But recently, I've felt God prompting me to stop saying those words and to instead set my mind like flint on Him and His strength to get me through.

Last year marked my third year in a row that I didn't pass out after getting blood drawn, and I finally got that nine-year-old cavity filled—in fact, two in one day! And I didn't even lose a wink of sleep.

—Rachael

CHAPTER 4

Fearful Thoughts and Words

Do not conform to the pattern of this world, but be transformed by the renewing of your mind. Then you will be able to test and approve what God's will is—his good, pleasing and perfect will.

Romans 12:2

Romans 12:2 teaches us that we cannot be transformed (changed) unless our minds are changed first. Some of the lessons I learned as I first began to study and receive God's Word were about my mind and thoughts. I was blessed to read an old book about the power of our thoughts and how the devil makes the mind a battlefield on which he wars with us by dropping untrue thoughts into our minds. He then attempts to get us to believe them so they will control our lives.

I had spent my life believing things that were not true according to God's Word. As a result, those lies had become my reality.

I realized that I had spent my life believing things that were not true according to God's Word. As a result, those lies had become my reality. I'll give you a few examples:

- I believed that somehow it was my fault that my father had sexually abused me.

- I believed I would always have a second-rate life because of the abuse.
- I believed something was wrong with me, and this recording played in my mind constantly: "What's wrong with me? What's wrong with me? What's wrong with me?"
- I believed that in order to avoid being hurt again, I had to have control of every situation and relationship.
- I believed that something bad was always right around the corner for me, and I lived with a fearful expectation of disappointment, bad news, or loss.
- I expected to be abandoned by men and any friends I had because that had been my experience in life.

I believed many other things that were not true, but I was deceived. To be deceived simply means to believe a lie. I believed lies, and those lies formed my reality. I think I can safely say that we all have times when we believe things that are not true because deceptive thoughts have become strongholds in our lives. Thoughts, whether they are true or false, positive or negative, build strongholds in our minds. Strongholds are places where our enemy, the devil, hides in order to destroy God's good plans for us.

Renewing the mind takes time and work. The only thing that overturns the lies we believe is the truth of God's Word. If we continue in God's Word, it makes us free (John 8:32). It doesn't make us free by simply reading it, but as we obey it we gain freedom a little bit at a time. I have been a student of God's Word for more than forty years, and I am still discovering little lies that I believe and working with the Holy Spirit to learn the truth so I can be free in yet another area of my life.

You may be of the opinion that your thoughts don't matter that much, but they are such an important force in your life. Thoughts become words, and words become attitudes and actions. Paul told the Colossians to set their minds "and keep them set" on things above, not on things of the earth (Col. 3:2 AMPC). This tells me that we have the ability to think about what we want to think about. We are not prisoners of whatever ideas happen to fall into our heads.

Another scripture that makes this truth clear is 2 Corinthians 10:4–6, which says that we should cast down wrong thoughts and imaginations and make them "obedient to Christ," or line up our thinking according to God's Word. This means that we can cast down one thought and think another on purpose. We are not captive to our thoughts; we can make them captive to us.

I used to believe, as many people do, that I had no control over what I thought. I never questioned where my thoughts came from; I simply accepted whatever I thought as truth and lived by it. What about you? What have you done in the past about your thoughts? You have probably done the same thing I did; most people do until they learn that their thoughts may be ruining their lives.

I have had the privilege of writing a book titled *The Battlefield of the Mind*. It was written in 1995 and is still one of my best-selling books because it helps people in such a practical way. Over the years, our office has received many testimonies of how people have been dramatically changed by learning that they could think their own thoughts. I encourage people to think about what they are thinking about. That may sound strange, but the next time you start to feel discouraged, depressed, or anxious, you will find the source of your problem if you will think about what you have been thinking about. Happy thoughts make us happy people.

I also wrote a book titled *Power Thoughts*, in which I teach people how to purposefully think thoughts that add power to their lives, such as, *I can do whatever I need to do in life through Christ, who is my strength. I love people, and I love to give and be generous. I will not live in fear because God is with me.* There are thousands of other thoughts like these. You can fill your mind with them daily, and they will empower you and help you be the person God wants you to be and do the things He wants you to do.

Take time each day to have "think sessions" when you take time to think some things on purpose that you want to see happen in your life. God's Word says that as a person "thinks in his heart, so is he" (Prov. 23:7 AMPC). In other words, where the mind goes, the person follows. Our thoughts chart the course our lives will take.

No matter how many years your thinking may have caused problems for you, you can renew your mind. It can be changed. And when your mind is changed, you will also change. I encourage you to set a goal to always think positive, hopeful, faith-filled thoughts. Believe the best about people rather than being suspicious and focusing on their faults, and it will improve your relationships greatly.

Imagination

The ability to imagine things that are not yet a reality is powerful. We can see pictures in our minds. For example, if I say "pink elephant," you immediately see a picture in your mind of a pink elephant. In our imagination, just as in our other thoughts, we should choose to imagine something wonderful. I encourage you to practice imagining great things that are impossible to you but are possible with God. Ask yourself, "Where do I see myself five years from now?" Or, "How do I believe God is calling me to make a difference in the world?"

God gave us the ability to imagine just as He gave us the ability to think, and He wants us to use it wisely. People who imagine great things end up doing great things. Before an automobile ever existed, someone had to imagine that it could be invented and actually think about it, probably for a long time. Someone designed the first chair. That person may have grown tired of sitting on a hard rock and said, "Surely there is something better to sit on than a rock, something soft and comfortable, something I can lean back on and relax." Then they must have imagined an example of what that could be and ultimately tried to build a seat with four legs and a back.

Thousands of people have good ideas but never do anything with them. Just imagining something is not good enough. We have to add effort to the imagination. Most important, we cannot be afraid to try. You must be willing to fail to find out if you can succeed. I have heard that Thomas Edison failed two thousand times while trying to create the light bulb. I don't know if that is accurate or not, but he obviously didn't create the light bulb perfectly the first time he tried. Instead of giving up, he said that each failure taught him what wouldn't work, and then he was able to eliminate that approach and go on to the next idea. Just because a person fails at something, it doesn't make him a failure. Nobody is a failure if they keep trying.

> *You must be willing to fail to find out if you can succeed.*

When God called me into ministry, I heard Him speak in my

heart that I would go around the world and teach His Word. For the first five years of my ministry, I taught a Bible study for approximately twenty-five people once a week in my living room. While I was teaching that small group, I imagined myself teaching large crowds of people. Today those large crowds are a reality in my life. Praying for God to do big things in your life is not helpful if your thoughts and imaginations are the opposite of what you have asked for.

I do not believe we can merely imagine anything we want and get it, but I do believe we need to keep our thoughts and imaginations in line with God's Word and His will for our lives. We can't walk with God unless we are in agreement with Him (Amos 3:3). So let me ask you: Are your thoughts and imaginations in agreement with God?

Thoughts Become Words, Attitudes, and Actions

When we receive the fearful thoughts the devil suggests to our minds and meditate on them, they become unhealthy attitudes. Try as we may to hide a bad attitude, it always sneaks out somewhere for others to see. Thoughts and attitudes become words we speak and actions we take.

If I meditate on how much a certain person has hurt me and how I am afraid they will do it again, and I plan to avoid them in order to protect myself and punish them, I am preparing for action. I will more than likely talk to someone about the way I feel, and my words may poison that person's attitude toward the one who hurt me. That is sad because they may really like the person.

Let's say that I am in church and the person who wounded me (and probably doesn't even realize the pain they caused) approaches me with a friendly attitude and invites me to lunch. It will be almost impossible for me to be friendly toward them or to not have a noticeably bad attitude. I might even explode verbally, ranting about how they hurt me, and blah, blah, blah! That person is likely to apologize and say they didn't even realize they had hurt me. Then I will go home, and at first I'll feel vindicated. But when my emotions calm down, I will realize that I grieved the Holy Spirit and most likely spend days feeling guilty. The next time I see the person, I will be embarrassed and want to run and hide, because that is what fear does, it runs and hides.

But let's think about another way this story could play out. Someone hurts me and the devil offers me fearful thoughts, making me think they hurt me on purpose and will probably do it again. He then offers me a thought suggesting I cut that person out of my life and find a way to get revenge. However, I have been studying God's Word, and I remember reading that love always believes the best of people (1 Cor. 13:4–7), so I cast down that bad thought and choose to believe the one who hurt me didn't even realize what happened. Perhaps the person felt bad physically, was going through a difficult time, or had just received bad news. Whatever the case, I choose to let the offense go and keep walking in love because I know that is what Jesus wants me to do.

I have a choice, and it is easy to see which choice is best.

Jesus said that whatever is in our hearts comes out of our mouths (Matt. 12:34). People often rationalize inappropriate remarks by saying, "I didn't mean it; I was just joking." They are only fooling themselves, because they may regret their comments, but the comments simply reflected what was in their hearts. They may have underlying thoughts and attitudes that pervaded their minds for a long time without even realizing what they allowed into their lives.

For us to walk in victory or enjoy the life Jesus died to give us, we must understand the power of words and work diligently with the Holy Spirit to learn to control what comes out of our mouths. This requires controlling our thoughts. We cannot control our words or our thoughts without the grace of God, but when we want to do the right thing and ask for His help, He always gives grace and more grace to help us.

I want to expound on a couple of powerful scriptures about the power of words.

First, let's look at Proverbs 18:20–21:

> From the fruit of their mouth a person's stomach is filled; with the harvest of their lips they are satisfied. The tongue has the power of life and death, and those who love it will eat its fruit.

We should take time to think deeply about what these two verses are saying. First, we will be satisfied or dissatisfied with our lives, at least partially, based on the words we speak. We not only speak words, but we also hear the words we speak, and they feed us. You have probably heard someone say at some time, "You will eat those words!" This means they will eventually regret what they have said. And we actually do eat our words in the sense that they go into our hearts. If they are good words, they bless us. If not, they poison our attitudes and steal our peace and joy. Just as people can get food poisoning from eating something rotten, we can get "word poisoning" if we allow rotten words to come out of our mouths.

"You will eat those words!"

We should also take time to look over and meditate on the words of the second verse of this passage: "The tongue has the power of life and death." Just imagine, we can speak life to ourselves and other people, or we can speak death.

We will eat the fruit of our words!

Next, let's look at James 3:2–10:

> We all stumble in many ways. Anyone who is never at fault in what they say is perfect, able to keep their whole body in check. When we put bits into the mouths of horses to make them obey us, we can turn the whole animal. Or take ships as an example. Although they are so large and are driven by strong winds, they are steered by a very small rudder wherever the pilot wants to go. Likewise, the tongue is a small part of the body, but it makes great boasts. Consider what a great forest is set on fire by a small spark. The tongue also is a fire, a world of evil among the parts of the body. It corrupts the whole body, sets the whole course of one's life on fire, and is itself set on fire by hell. All kinds of animals, birds, reptiles and sea creatures are being tamed and have been tamed by mankind, but no human being can tame the tongue. It is a restless evil, full of deadly poison. With the tongue we praise our Lord and Father, and with it we curse human beings, who have been made in God's likeness. Out of the same mouth come praise and cursing. My brothers and sisters, this should not be.

These scriptures teach us that the words we speak determine the direction of our lives. I said earlier that both God and the devil have a plan for our lives. The plan we follow is the one we agree with. Our words reveal what is in our hearts, and in some unguarded moment what we truly believe will slip out, revealing what is in our hearts if we will learn to listen to ourselves.

Let's say the same things God says no matter what we think, how we feel, or how things look. You and I have a profound effect on our future. If we speak positively in agreement with God, we will have positive outcomes.

No one can get anything they want simply by saying they will have it, but we can have what God wants us to have if we agree and cooperate with Him. If we think fear and speak fear, we prevent ourselves from making progress in life. We are imprisoned by our own thoughts and words. Instead of saying, "I'm afraid," learn to say, "When I feel fear, I will do it afraid."

Don't pray for tasks equal to your powers. Pray for power equal to your tasks.

Phillips Brooks

Anything Is Possible with God

For forty years, I lived with a crippling fear of buses, planes, and large crowds. I know—that eliminates a lot of life! Even though I knew the fear was irrational, I just couldn't take that first step toward breaking free from it. Then a few years ago, I began studying what God's Word says about fear. The more I learned, the more I prayed for God's help to be free in this area.

Soon after, I was asked to chaperone my daughter's kindergarten field trip to an apple orchard. I knew it would mean getting on a bus—with *other people*. I said yes and prayed it would be canceled.

The day came and I was faced with the big yellow monster. Body shaking, I stepped onto the bus and sat down. In my mind, I began to focus on specific scriptures that would help me—passages such as Psalm 91—and even spoke them softly under my breath. Soon, the fifteen-minute trip was over. I felt like I had climbed a mountain!

My next challenge was much bigger—attending a Christian conference held at a stadium in a neighboring city. Year after year, I had signed up, but then backed out at the last minute. *Not this year.*

The weekend came, and I drove into town with friends. But when the shuttle bus came, I stood paralyzed. I wanted to turn and go home. Then I said to myself, "Shawn, if you don't do this, you'll go back to being afraid all the time."

I stepped on the bus, then minutes later stepped into a stadium with thousands of people. After about five minutes, something amazing happened: *I wasn't afraid anymore.*

About a year later, I faced my "final exam"—a mission trip to India. I knew God had called me to go, but it required five airplanes and several buses to get there. I wanted to turn around several times, but the Lord kept saying, "One step at a time. Just take what's in front of you."

I finally arrived at one of the busiest airports in the world, *and I wasn't overwhelmed.* God showed me that with Him, anything is possible.

—Shawn

CHAPTER 5

I "Feel" Afraid

When I am afraid, I put my trust in you.

Psalm 56:3

The feeling of fear is very real. It can even manifest physically. I believe fear can make us shake and sweat, make our hearts beat faster, interrupt our normal breathing, and provoke other physical symptoms. But we can manage these sensations realistically if we remember that they are just feelings and that the fear of something bad happening is usually worse than actually dealing with a situation that threatens us. Remember: Fear holds us back and prevents us from making progress in our lives.

If I am afraid I will hurt myself when I try to exercise, I won't exercise. I know this because I really did hurt myself trying to exercise, and I used that one bad experience to avoid exercising for years. The reason I hurt myself was that I tried to do too much too quickly and had poor posture while trying to lift weights. That is a recipe for injury! What I needed was a trainer to teach me the basics of proper exercise. Eventually, I began working with a trainer, and I have done that for years now. Regular exercise has helped me tremendously.

Fear can steal anything from us if we let it. I wish I knew how many fears I have not located, yet they are hiding somewhere in my life. In God's timing, He will show me. Thankfully, God doesn't reveal everything we need to deal with all at once. If He did, we would be overwhelmed and give up before we ever got started.

Early in my ministry, I was praying and asking God to send me invitations to speak at conferences and in churches. I had been praying for a while, but nothing had happened. Then, finally, two opportunities came about the same time. The first one was in Colorado. A well-known minister was scheduled to speak ahead of me, so that pretty much guaranteed a good crowd, and I was glad about that. As it turned out, he had to cancel for some reason at the last moment, which left only me, someone nobody knew. The crowd was discouragingly small.

I went straight from there to Florida, where I had been invited at the last minute to fill in for someone who couldn't make it. I was asked because someone who knew someone knew someone who knew me and suggested me as a speaker. The conference organizers asked me to speak in an afternoon session; I was not one of the main speakers, but I was thrilled to have any opportunity at all.

At that event, the front row was filled with speakers—Doctor So-and-So, Bishop So-and-So, a prophet from Africa, and a well-known reverend. Then there was me, just plain Joyce. No fancy title, not known or sought after, but there I sat about to get my prayer answered. And I was scared stiff, as they say. I guess that means to be so frightened that you can barely move, which was how I felt. I felt insignificant, little, ridiculous—as though I should go back home and never leave again.

Then it happened: Before the main speaker spoke that night, the organizer of the conference asked each workshop speaker to take a few minutes to tell what they planned to talk about the next day. I had already spent the day imagining my workshop being totally empty!

I stood to speak for those few minutes and was so fearful that when I opened my mouth to talk, my voice barely squeaked. I felt like a fool. I had a decision to make: I could gather all my courage, try again, and hope for the best, or I could run off the platform (which is what I felt like doing) and flee home to St. Louis as fast as I could get there.

Well, I did open my mouth again. I still remember that I was going to speak from Galatians 3:1–3 the next day, teaching people about how we cannot change ourselves by works, but we can humble ourselves and receive God's grace to do the work that needs to be done. The next day my workshop was packed. There were no seats left, and people were standing in the back of the room. I'm still here today, speaking at conferences, in churches, and on television and radio. Fear tried to steal my destiny, and it almost succeeded. I had to confront fear, and so will you. Don't let fear stop you, because if you do, you will miss amazing opportunities that God has prearranged for you to enjoy (Eph. 2:10).

Understanding Feelings

I doubt that any of us will ever understand all of our feelings, because they can be quite mysterious. Feelings can be very good, and they can be very bad. They seem to come and go at their own discretion. I like to say that they are fickle—they change often and without notice.

> I doubt that any of us will ever understand all of our feelings, because they can be quite mysterious.

For example, on a Sunday morning at church when the pastor talks about the importance of children and how badly they need people to volunteer to work in the nursery, I can easily "feel" that I want to do that. I am excited. I want to serve. I am sure I won't mind not being in the adult service or working in the nursery during the early service and then staying so I can enjoy the later service. I might even be excited the first time I do it, but after listening to crying babies, changing smelly diapers, and dealing with ungrateful parents or parents who complain, don't be surprised if I no longer "feel" like I want to work in the nursery.

People who understand the importance of making commitments and keeping their word will move past their feelings and take action anyway. Unfortunately, many others would simply not return to the nursery and justify their lack of follow-through by thinking it is not what God wants them to do. If He had wanted them to do it, they reason, they would have enjoyed it. While I don't believe God calls us to do things we are miserable doing for the rest of our lives, I do believe and know from experience that we may be called upon to do some things that are not that exciting for us, but they represent a need we can meet. I think sometimes these are tests from God designed to teach us the importance of keeping our word. The Bible says a godly person "swears to his own hurt and does not change" (Ps. 15:4 ESV). To me this means that even if we say we will do something and later wish we had not committed to do it, we still need to keep our word. It's wise to pray and think about making a commitment before saying yes.

More than anything else these days, people seem to talk about how they feel, so obviously, we place a great deal of dependence on feelings. However, it is not wise to make feelings—or the lack of feelings—the criteria by which we judge a matter. I wrote a book titled *Living beyond Your Feelings*, which explores this more fully. As with fear, there are other feelings that try to dictate our behavior. We can learn to not allow these emotions to rule our decisions. Understanding how unstable feelings are has helped me learn not to depend on them too much.

Think about your job or career, as an example. As of the writing of this book, I have been teaching God's Word for forty-three years, and for thirty-three of those years I have traveled doing conferences and speaking engagements. I recall someone asking me how I felt about all the travel I need to do, and I answered, "I haven't asked myself about that in a long time."

We should stop asking ourselves how we feel about doing what we know we should do. If we don't stop consulting our feelings, we will not finish many things in life.

At first, traveling in ministry was exciting to me; however, my enthusiasm for it soon waned with all the packing and unpacking, sleeping on mattresses that are not always comfortable, dirty carpets with stains, refrigerators that freeze everything you put in them, noise from the room next door, music from the patio bar that happens to be right under your window, and other inconveniences. Of course, not every travel experience has been negative. There are many lovely hotels, but hotels are not home, so it is easy to get tired of them.

I've done thousands of speaking engagements and conferences over the years, and someone asked me a few months ago if I was excited about one that was coming up. When I said no, that person looked at me like I had committed the unpardonable sin. Realizing the shock and disappointment that individual felt, I quickly explained that although I wasn't emotionally excited, I was very committed to the conference and would be committed to teaching God's Word as long as I was alive. If we can understand this and purpose to do what we need to do whether we feel like it or not, we are well on our way to victory.

No matter what we do, when the newness wears off it will no longer excite us. If we don't know how to switch gears from excitement to commitment, we will bounce around from one thing to another all of our lives and not finish much of anything. The apostle Paul said that it was very important to him to complete what God had called him to do:

> No matter what we do, when the newness wears off it will no longer excite us.

> But *none of these things move me*; neither do I esteem my life dear to myself, if only I may finish my course *with joy*.
>
> Acts 20:24 AMPC

Paul was unmoved by persecution, inconvenience, and difficulty. He had made his mind up to finish the call on his life, which was to preach the gospel by the grace of God. He wanted to do that with joy, but joy is different from emotional excitement. I had joy about doing the conference I was asked about. I was very happy for the people who would be there and what they would learn, but I wasn't emotionally excited.

Emotional excitement gives us actual energy, but we eventually have to learn to live by determination to finish what God has given us to do and trust Him for the energy needed to perform the task.

Dependence on excitement is one reason the divorce rate in our society is so high. We are a bit addicted to entertainment and excitement, and when a marriage is no longer exciting, some people want to move on to someone else who will excite them. But that kind of relationship will not last, either. I often say I don't get chills when Dave comes home, nor does my heart beat faster, but I do deeply love him and am committed to him "until death do us part." As I'm writing this book, we have been married fifty-three years, and a commitment like that requires more than emotional excitement.

There is nothing evil about excitement. If we feel it, we should enjoy it, but we must also learn not to depend on it, because it comes and goes.

Jesus also talked about the fact that He had finished what His Father sent Him to do (John 17:4), but I doubt seriously that being crucified was exciting. The Bible says that He endured the cross, despising the shame of it, for the joy that was set before Him (Heb. 12:2). It feels really good when we know that we have finished what God has asked us to do.

As my parents, who had abused and abandoned me, got too old to properly care for themselves, the Lord asked me to take care of them. After a good deal of arguing with Him, which of course is useless, I said yes. I didn't realize at the time that they would live another thirteen years and require a lot of expensive and time-consuming care. It wasn't exciting or fun for me, but I did it because I knew it was the right thing to do. I am so joyful now in knowing that I finished the job God gave me to do.

If you have lost your enthusiasm or excitement about something, don't give up simply for that reason. Before you quit anything, make sure God is telling you to do so. Even though He might ask you to do something difficult, He will give you the grace to do it. Our answer to anything He asks us to do should always be yes.

> If you have lost your enthusiasm or excitement about something, don't give up simply for that reason.

Instead of making decisions based on whether or not you feel afraid, make them based on being courageous. According to Karle Wilson Baker's short poem "Courage," "Courage is Fear that has said its prayers" and gone forward to do what it was asked to do.

Of all the liars in the world, sometimes the worst are our own fears.

Rudyard Kipling

The Tiger's Roar

One of the most majestic of all creatures is the tiger. For many years these big beautiful creatures have puzzled researchers. It seems that when tigers hunt, they have a remarkable capacity for paralyzing their prey with fear, a capacity greater than any of the other big cats. As the tiger charges toward its hapless prey, it lets out a spine-chilling roar. Now you'd think this would be enough to cause the prey to turn and run for its life, but instead it often freezes and soon becomes tiger food.

At the turn of this century, scientists discovered why you're likely to freeze to the spot rather than run when the tiger charges. When the tiger roars, it lets out sound waves that are audible—the ones that sound terrifying. It also lets out sound at a frequency so low you can't hear it, but you can feel it. And so, as the tiger emerges from the undergrowth, the flashing of its colors, the sound of its roar, and the impact of the unheard but felt sound waves combine to provide an all-out assault on your senses. The effect is that you are momentarily paralyzed, so even though there may be time to avoid the tiger, you are tricked into standing still long enough for the tiger to leap on you.

Our fears often operate in the same way. They paralyze us into inactivity, even when the real threat is not immediately upon us. Part of overcoming the challenges before us is recognizing the ability for our fear of what might happen to stop us from dealing well with the challenge.

CHAPTER 6

Why Am I Afraid?

Be alert and of sober mind. Your enemy the devil prowls around like a roaring lion looking for someone to devour.

1 Peter 5:8

We may easily forget about the devil because we cannot see him. We blame our problems on other people, ourselves, circumstances, and even God, but in many cases these troubles are actually the work of the devil. Although Satan can work through people and circumstances, he is the root of many of our problems. He is our adversary, our enemy, the one who is always against us, constantly trying to hinder and steal God's good plan for our lives. Remember that John 10:10 says the devil comes for three reasons: to steal, to kill, and to destroy.

Discovering that Satan is real and was the source of my problems was a life-changer for me. I was a Christian, but one who had no victory in my life, and I accepted whatever came along as either God's will or the fault of someone who simply would not do what I wanted them to do to make me happy. I blamed my problems on anyone and anything except the devil because although I understood there is a devil and that evil does exist in the world, I didn't see him as a personal influence in my life.

You may be in that same place where I once was. Take a few minutes and view the devil as the Bible verse above describes him: an adversary, an enemy who prowls around, always lurking around somewhere close to you, seeking an opening into your life so he can devour your peace, joy, and victory.

It is possible for us to allow the devil to influence us. Paul warned us in Ephesians 4:26–27 not to give the devil a foothold in our lives. This passage indicates that the devil can gain a foothold through unresolved anger, but there are other ways we can also give him access to us.

One way we let the devil take advantage of us is through fear. In fact, I believe fear is the number one weapon he uses against us. Sadly, we usually accept that as something we cannot do anything about. We think we are just afraid and that is all there is to it. We assume we are incapable of making progress or doing the things we truly want to do because we are fearful for some reason. I believed for years that I was simply a coward because I was afraid, but thank God I learned to "do it afraid." That one idea brought wonderful change into my life. We are not cowards because we feel fear; we are only cowards if we submit to the fear and do as it instructs, which means we do nothing or we run and hide.

Fear is the number one weapon the enemy uses against us.

Although people often don't like to hear about the devil because it isn't a pleasant subject, learning how to break free from fear is impossible unless we realize that the devil is the source of all fear.

> For God gave us a spirit not of fear but of power and love and self-control.
>
> 2 Timothy 1:7 ESV

Since fear is not from God, it must be from the devil. God gives us faith, and the devil counteracts with fear. The only force that overcomes fear is faith, and faith sees and listens to God and takes action while it still feels afraid.

> Submit yourselves therefore to God. Resist the devil, and
> he will flee from you.
>
> James 4:7 ESV

We must resist the devil or he will ruin our lives with his lies if we believe them. We are to stand firm against the devil, be strong, and be watchful to make sure he does not devour us.

Jesus resisted the devil when Peter attempted to talk Him out of going to the cross (Matt. 16:23). He said, essentially, "Get behind me, Satan; you are a hindrance, and you're in my way." Satan was actually using Peter to try to convince Jesus to disobey God. He often uses the people closest to us to derail us from our destiny. They do not purposefully attempt to get us to disobey God, but they do want us to do what they want us to do, not what God or anyone else wants us to do. Peter didn't want Jesus to suffer and die, so he told Him not to go to the place where He would suffer. But Jesus rebuked Peter, knowing that the devil was actually working through him, trying to stop Him from fulfilling God's plan.

If we are going to resist the devil, we must resist taking the action fear demands that we take or don't take. If fear says, "You cannot do that; you will make a fool of yourself," you should say, "I can do all things through Christ who strengthens me" (Phil. 4:13 NKJV) and then take the necessary action, even though you feel afraid.

Conquer through Confrontation

We can pray to be delivered from fear, but often, instead of removing feelings of fear, God gives us the courage to confront the fear and move forward. God told Joshua to fear not but to be courageous (Josh. 1:5, 9). He was warning Joshua that fear would try to stop him from taking the Promised Land, but that if he would be courageous, no matter how he felt, it would bring great victory.

Unless evil is confronted it will always prevail. The longer it goes without being confronted, the more territory it takes and the stronger it becomes. Our society today is filled with evil. If we do nothing to stop it, then in essence, we are agreeing with it. You might ask what you can do. One thing you can do is speak out against it, because silence is agreement.

> Our society today is filled with evil. If we do nothing to stop it, then in essence, we are agreeing with it.

Every Believer Has Authority over Satan

Don't think that others might be able to exercise authority over the devil because they are somehow "special" believers, but that you don't have that privilege.

> Behold, I give unto you power to tread on serpents and scorpions, and over all the power of the enemy: and nothing shall by any means hurt you.
>
> Luke 10:19 KJV

This scripture isn't written to only "super saints"; it is written to all believers in Jesus Christ. God has given us power and authority, but it doesn't do us any good if we do not exercise it.

We exercise it by resisting the devil, speaking against him and his works, and refusing to believe his lies. When Satan lied to Jesus, He always responded by quoting back to him a scripture that refuted his lie (Luke 4:1–10). We should also talk back to the devil. The Bible says, "Let the one who has my word speak it faithfully" (Jer. 23:28).

Every time you feel afraid, remember that the fear is coming from Satan. The only right kind of fear is the reverential fear of God, which is an awe-inspiring, respectful type of fear that gives Him honor above all else. Scripture refers to this as "the fear of the Lord." The fear of the Lord is not intended to make us afraid that God will harm us. God is always good, but through our own foolishness we can open doors for the devil by disobeying God. For this reason, Scripture urges us to have a reverential fear of God. This attitude toward Him will keep us on the right path in life and prevent us from thinking that disobeying Him is no big deal. We can be forgiven for our sins, but doing the right thing to start with is even better. Proverbs 9:10 says, "The fear of the Lord is the beginning of wisdom."

Some situations call for wisdom in the form of legitimate caution or concern, such as a fire, going out into deep water (unless we are great swimmers), going to bed with our doors unlocked, enduring physical pain or unusual symptoms for a year and not going to the doctor, or walking out into the middle of traffic where there is no stop sign. Many people get hurt simply because they don't use common sense, but then common sense isn't very common these days. I believe wisdom is sanctified common sense. God has given us wisdom, but we must use it in order to benefit from it.

There are a few fears that are good ones because they keep us from being harmed; however, the fears that prevent us from doing what we believe we should do, or even things that we want to do, are all from the devil.

No Longer a Victim

Many people who have been hurt or taken advantage of spend their lives with a victim mentality. I urge you not to do that. If the devil has managed to hurt you once, don't allow him to keep hurting you by accepting the lie that you are a victim. You may have been a victim at one time, but as a child of God you are now a new creature, and old things have passed away (2 Cor. 5:17). I was sexually abused during my childhood, but I feel now that all of that happened to someone I used to know, because I am no longer that helpless victim. I am a new person in Christ, and so are you. We are more than conquerors through Christ, who loves us (Rom. 8:37).

God's Word teaches us to give no place to the devil (Eph. 4:27). We can give place to him in a variety of ways. Ephesians 4:27 speaks specifically of holding on to anger and refusing to forgive as a way of giving place to the devil, but wrong attitudes can produce the same results. For many years, even as a Christian, I had a bitter, self-pitying, unforgiving attitude while God was offering me power. But I came to realize that I could not keep my bad attitudes and also have His power. I had a reason to feel sorry for myself, and perhaps you do also, but we have no right to feel that way because Jesus died for us in order to set us free from the past and enable us to live brand-new lives.

> I could not keep my bad attitudes and also have God's power.

Satan Torments

Many of the fears and phobias people experience are designed for no other reason than to torment them. There are so many types of phobias that there is no way to list them, but each one seems very real to the person who suffers from it. Just to list a few, we have fears of public speaking, heights, small spaces, crowds, clowns, germs, the dark, storms, snakes, and spiders. Jerry Seinfeld once said, "One of the great mysteries to me is the fact that a woman could pour hot wax on her legs, rip the hair out by the roots, and still be afraid of a spider."

Some phobias are especially unusual, like nomophobia, which is the fear of being without your mobile phone or being unable to use mobile devices. I feel very bad for people who are so tormented by any of these fears, but I do believe the only way to get over them is to confront them. Some people need counseling or therapy from a professional. Whatever you need to do, I urge you not to merely put up with fear and let it control you.

God wants to bless you, and He wants you to have peace and great joy. When you feel fear, immediately put your trust in God and do it afraid!

Resist your fear; fear will never lead you to a positive end.
Go for your faith and what you believe.

T. D. Jakes

Facing Fear Together

For as long as I can remember, I was afraid of the dark. As a young girl and teenager, I would lie in bed petrified, listening for noises. Time and again, I would yell for my parents, forcing them to look through the house and assure me that everything was safe.

When I finally managed to fall asleep, it wasn't much better. I was often tormented by nightmares, waking up in a panic.

I kept telling myself, *Surely, this will all go away when I get older.* But it never did. Every night, even as an adult, I turned into that same eight-year-old girl, cowering under the blankets, listening for noises.

My fear of the dark followed me into my thirties. Even as a married woman, I routinely woke my husband, Tom, to look around the house and try to calm my fears. I was humiliated, but I didn't know what else to do.

Then, just when I didn't think it could get any worse, Tom was asked to work nights at his job. I came face-to-face with my greatest fear: being alone in the dark.

Around that time I began developing a closer relationship with God. I asked Him what I should do about my intense fear. I'll never forget what He spoke to my heart: "We will face the fear of darkness together."

The Lord led me to begin memorizing scriptures about fear. At night, as I sat in my bed, I would pray in the Spirit and speak various scriptures aloud: "God has not given me a spirit of fear, but of power, love, and a sound mind! When I lay down, I will not be afraid, but my sleep shall be sweet" (2 Tim. 1:7; Prov. 3:24).

I continued to pray, filled my mind with His Word, and spoke it as often as I could. Gradually, God performed a miracle and broke the power of fear that had been my companion for so long. After all those years, I was finally able to say, "I'm not afraid of the dark."

—Donna

CHAPTER 7

The Antidote for Fear

*There is no fear in love. But perfect love drives out fear,
because fear has to do with punishment. The one who fears
is not made perfect in love.*

1 John 4:18

You have read that one reason we don't have to be afraid is that
we know God is always with us. Another major reason we don't
need to live in fear is that God loves us perfectly. As long as we
allow fear to rule us, we still need to keep learning about and
experiencing God's love for us.

Because God loves us, He will always take good care of us and
help us. We can be confident and secure in the knowledge that
He loves us all the time, in every situation. The apostle Paul said
we should be so rooted in God's love that nothing, no matter how
bad it seems, is able to separate us from it:

> Who shall separate us from the love of Christ? Shall
> trouble or hardship or persecution or famine or nakedness
> or danger or sword?...No, in all these things we are
> more than conquerors through him who loved us. For
> I am convinced that neither death nor life, nor angels
> nor demons, neither the present nor the future, nor any

> powers, neither height nor depth, nor anything else in all creation, will be able to separate us from the love of God that is in Christ Jesus our Lord.
>
> Romans 8:35, 37–39

Notice that Paul said he was "sure" that nothing could separate us from God's love. We can have confidence in that. Thinking often about how much God loves you will help you confront the fears in your life. It is easy to tell others that God loves them, but it gets more difficult when we think about His loving us. The devil definitely doesn't want you to know the perfect love of God that flows continually toward you because he knows it will make you strong, fearless, secure, and confident.

Insecurity

Insecure people are self-focused. They are continually concerned about what other people think of them, and the fears they experience are endless. They cannot develop good relationships because they stay busy trying to impress other people instead of being good friends to them.

It really makes me sad when I deal with a person who is insecure, because everything they do and think and decide is colored by their insecurities. They turn down opportunities due to fears of inadequacy, and their insecurities make other people doubt that they can depend on them. The cure for the insecure is receiving the love of God. It is like a healing ointment that heals the soul (inner life), and I personally think it is the only thing that can

> The cure for the insecure is receiving the love of God.

do that. Everybody wants to be loved, but we often look for love in all the wrong places while ignoring God's love, which is being poured out on us all the time (Rom. 5:5).

As Christians we may hear frequently that God loves us, but are we really listening, and do we understand the amazing power of His love? Understanding something with our minds is quite different from hearing it with our hearts and actually believing and receiving it. I remember standing in front of a mirror, looking myself in the eye, and saying out loud, "Joyce, God loves you!" I thought about those words and spoke them over myself often until that truth became a reality in my life.

When your prayers haven't been answered the way you hoped, or when you have experienced pain, loss, or tragedy, have you ever said, "God, don't You love me?" I know I have, and you may have also, but I never say that now because I know that nothing can separate us from God's love.

When we are insecure, we have lots of fears, many of which are about ourselves. The relationship we have with ourselves is vitally important, and we should prioritize making that relationship healthy, because if we don't like who we are and feel guilty most of the time due to our imperfections, it will cause us to never be able to truly enjoy life. I will even go so far as to say we should love ourselves. When I make that assertion, most people put a wall up and immediately think it reflects a selfish and self-centered attitude that cannot possibly be right. Religion has taught us so much about being sinners that we may fail to remember that we are also forgiven and made new in Christ. Of course we should grieve over our sin and seek

> *Religion has taught us so much about being sinners that we may fail to remember that we are also forgiven.*

to overcome it, but even in the midst of our worst moments, God still loves us. Receiving His love means that we love ourselves in a balanced way, not a selfish or self-centered way.

I had a friend who hated herself, and I recall a time when she asked the pastor of our church to pray for her. When he asked what she needed prayer for, she replied, "I hate myself." The pastor took a couple of steps back and looked right at her and said, "Who do you think you are? You have no right to hate yourself, because Jesus suffered greatly because of His great love for you. One way to offer thanks to Him is to receive His love and love yourself."

We are to be unselfish and always desire to help others, but we can do that and still love ourselves in a godly way. As a matter of fact, I find that the more I value myself and am at peace with myself, the more I want to forget myself and help those in need. I urge you to come to terms of peace with yourself and appreciate the unique person God created you to be.

There is a difference between being in love with ourselves and loving ourselves because God created us and loves us with a perfect love. To love oneself is to receive God's love. He values us and wants us to value ourselves. Have you ever tried to compliment someone who has no ability to simply receive your kind words humbly and say thank you? I have, and it is like getting slapped in the face. I imagine it hurts God, too, when He pours His love out to us and we don't receive it because we don't think we deserve it.

The reason Jesus came to redeem us is that we can never be good enough to deserve God's love. The Bible says that His love has been freely *poured* out on us through the Holy Spirit (Rom. 5:5). The prophet Malachi said that God pours out His blessings

(Mal. 3:10). We can see that God is not stingy and all He wants us to do is love Him and open our hearts to receive His goodness and love.

You may think you need to behave better and sin less before God can love you or bless you, but the truth is that the more you receive the love of God, the more you will love Him in return. Then, out of that love, you will want to obey Him. We don't obey God to get Him to love us, but in response to the fact that He does love us very much, even though we are completely undeserving of it.

I have gone through times with some friends, and with my children and grandchildren, when for one reason or another, even something as simple as a pimple made them feel really bad about themselves. When they felt that way, it really hurt me. I tried and tried to convince them they are wonderful, special, valued, and loved, but they were so engrossed in their faults that they refused to believe me. When I compare those experiences with how God must feel, I feel sad for Him because so many of His children reject His love.

Receive God's love and let it heal all your insecurities and give you the courage to face life boldly and do whatever you need to do, even if you have to do it afraid.

Are You Angry with Yourself?

I know a woman who was always angry about one thing or another. Although she appeared to be angry with other people, she was actually angry with herself. Being with her was uncomfortable and made people tense. She was a perfectionist with a list of things she expected from herself, and anytime she didn't measure up to her own expectations, she became angry. She felt bad about herself unless she succeeded at everything she did and was able to check every item off of her to-do list each day. She also felt good and proud on the rare occasions when she did accomplish all she had on her list and behaved all day in an exemplary manner. She bounced between pride and guilt—pride if she did well and guilt if she didn't. Does this sound familiar? A lot of people pressure themselves the same way she did until they finally realize they cannot buy God's love and approval, because no matter how perfect we may think we are, we always lack something. Jesus died for us when we were still in sin, so we can see that we did nothing to earn His love (Rom. 5:6–8).

> But because of his great love for us, God, who is rich in mercy, made us alive with Christ even when we were dead in transgressions.
>
> Ephesians 2:4–5

God's love is a gift, and the fact that He loves us so much that He sent His only Son, Jesus, to pay for our sins and suffer in our place is proof of that love.

I understand not liking oneself and being insecure, because I was that way at one time. I didn't appear to be an insecure person, but in my mind and heart I was. I needed my husband to always put me first in everything in his life and to want to be with me constantly. As a result, he felt suffocated and manipulated. The person I appeared to be to the world around me was not truly the person I was, and I could change quickly based on what people expected of me.

I remember Dave asking me one time, "Why do you become a totally different person when you are around your dad?" I wasn't even aware I did that, but he was right. I changed my behavior around my father because I was fearful and insecure around him. I had never confronted him about his sin against me, and I needed to do that in order to be free to be myself when I needed to be around him. Eventually I did, but it took a long time before I was willing to do it, and even when I did, it was with trembling and great fear of what his reaction would be. I can definitely say I did it afraid. Although his reaction was not positive, it was a step forward, and simply confronting my fear of him weakened that fear. I talked to him about the abuse again at a later time, and eventually he was able to repent and receive Jesus as his Savior.

Secure in Christ

God offers us security in Him. This scripture is a good example of that promise.

> He drew me up from the pit of destruction, out of the miry bog, and set my feet upon a rock, making my steps secure.
>
> Psalm 40:2 ESV

God is our deliverer, but we cannot be delivered from something if we refuse to admit it is a problem or if we use it as a crutch to control other people. I have heard too many people use "I can't help it, I'm insecure" as an excuse for not taking action when they should. We will never be free from anything we keep excusing.

We will never be free from anything we keep excusing.

When we receive Jesus as our Savior, it is not merely so we can go to heaven when we die, but so we can live in freedom and victory while we are on earth. Letting God set us free from the past and heal us is one way we glorify His name. We become trophies of His grace! He is an expert at healing the brokenhearted and making the fearful courageous.

The apostle Peter was so insecure and fearful that, when threatened, he denied three times that he even knew Christ (Luke 22:-54–62). But later, after the Holy Spirit had come upon him, he boldly preached in the streets of Jerusalem and about three thousand souls were added to the church that day (Acts 2:41). What a magnificent change! It shows how cowardly we can be if we depend on ourselves and how bold we can be if we depend on Jesus and His grace.

You will stay timid and fearful the remainder of your life unless you determine to be aggressive against fear and insecurity and refuse to be anything other than what God wants you to be. You are strong in the Lord and the power of His might (Eph. 6:10). Start seeing yourself as strong instead of weak and fearful, insecure, and timid. See yourself as someone who is loved unconditionally, valued and precious in God's sight. What you believe about yourself is very important. No matter how much God has done for us, if we don't believe it, we will never claim it as our own. We receive from God through faith and believing His Word, and we receive from the devil through fear and insecurity.

It is not God's will for you to be insecure. Insecurity is not just part of your personality, nor is it something you have to put up with. Learn how much God loves you, because it is the cure for the insecure, and it will make you bold.

> It is not God's will for you to be insecure. Insecurity is not just part of your personality, nor is it something you have to put up with.

God's love is not given in varying

degrees based on our level of so-called perfection. God is love. He loves us because He is kind and He wants to. No matter what you do, it won't stop God from loving you. It may stop you from receiving His love, but His love is always present to heal and deliver—no matter what.

The brave man is not he who does not feel afraid, but he who conquers that fear.

Nelson Mandela

Singing through the Fear

Fear seems to strike at the strangest times, in the strangest ways. For instance, if anyone had told me twenty years ago (when I was only eighteen) that I would one day be afraid to sing, I wouldn't have believed it!

Back then, I lived in Indonesia, where I was born and raised. I grew up singing in the choir, and I loved every minute of it. I even went on to sing professionally, working with popular music groups and performing on television. Singing was in my blood.

In my early twenties, I moved to the United States, where I met my husband. I eventually had our beautiful daughter, and for years I gladly placed singing on the back burner.

A few years ago, God began speaking to my heart about singing and leading worship. I was extremely hesitant. I told God, "If You want me to do this, the pastor himself will need to come ask me."

Of course, you know what happened next. After church one day, my pastor approached me and said, "I heard you can sing. Would you be interested?"

I told him yes, but I was *petrified*. I hadn't sung in years, and I was apprehensive about jumping back in. Plus, it's one thing to sing a pop song, but leading worship is totally different.

For the next two years, I led worship in some capacity at my church, *and it completely changed my life*. For starters, it was the beginning of a deeper, more fulfilling relationship with God.

But that bold decision to stand up there onstage—when I didn't know if I would fail or succeed—also gave me a new confidence in other areas. Shortly afterward, I made a bold decision at work to take on a new, more challenging role. That decision then led to even greater opportunities.

I can honestly say that I'm not the woman I used to be. I am bolder, more confident, and more apt to try new things. And it all began when I decided to do it afraid—and sing.

—Melanie

CHAPTER 8

Living Boldly

The wicked flee though no one pursues, but the righteous are as bold as a lion.

Proverbs 28:1

There is no power shortage in heaven, and God is not in a recession. He has more than enough for anything we need. Job said, "How great is God—beyond our understanding!" (Job 36:26).

All too often when we are faced with a challenge or an opportunity to do something we have never done before, we ask ourselves if we think we can do it. But that is entirely the wrong question. What we should ask is, "God, can You do it?" God is not asking us to do things; He is asking us to let Him do things through us.

I can assure you that you can do anything that God asks you to do, no matter how difficult it is or how much experience you lack, if you will keep your eyes on Him and realize He is more than enough. Don't let the devil steal your blessings through fear. What is impossible with human beings is possible with God (Luke 18:27).

> What eye has not seen and ear has not heard and has not entered into the heart of man, [all that] God has prepared (made and keeps ready) for those who love Him.
>
> 1 Corinthians 2:9 AMPC

This scripture tells us that we cannot even begin to imagine how much God wants to do for and through us if we will love Him and believe Him. Faith leads to boldness, and boldness leads to success. Boldness is the answer to fear. Fear will come, but boldness can chase it away. Peter had to get out of the boat in order to walk on water (Matt. 14:29). Joshua and the priests had to put their feet in the Jordan River before the waters parted (Josh. 3:5–17). And you and I will often have to take steps of action while we feel afraid. With each bold step we take, we come closer to reaching our goal.

The apostle Paul prayed for the believers in Ephesus to be enlightened so they would understand the greatness of God's power toward them (Eph. 1:18–19). We all need to do that. Paul didn't pray for the believers to have no challenges and no opposition; he prayed that they would know and understand the power available to them through Christ. We have all heard stories about a person who lived as a pauper, but when he died, a million dollars in cash was found hidden in his mattress. Let's make sure we are not like the millionaire who lived like a pauper, having all of God's resources available to us yet acting as though we have very little. I encourage you to refuse to do nothing, because power is available to do anything!

> *Refuse to do nothing, because power is available to do anything!*

God is able to do much more than we can ask, think, or imagine through His power that works in us (Eph. 3:20). Please notice this scripture says God does it through His power working *in* us. God doesn't do it for us.

Until we see and understand that God's power, not our human strength, is at work, we will be limited to doing what we think we have the ability to do and we will stop there. But with God as our partner in life, all things are possible. It is not only possible for us to do great things, but it is also possible to do hard things.

I know a young couple with two sets of twins, and the oldest two boys have autism. I am continually amazed at how they do what they do. I know another lovely couple who have a special needs child who requires almost constant care, and once again, I marvel at their ability. We often look at people going through very hard things and say or think, "I don't know how you can do it." Not only do they do it, but they do it with smiles on their faces. They don't complain, and even though their lives are quite busy, they find time to help others.

I recently heard a message delivered by a woman who had a severe stroke that left her with many physical problems. Her life was very hard, but she insisted it was good.

How Do They Do It?

How do people deal with such difficult situations? Sometimes I can't make it through a few hours without complaining about something so minor that it is ridiculous, but at other times I have gone through very difficult circumstances, and nobody even knew it except those closest to me.

The answer to how some people do what they do is this: by the grace (power) of God. Grace is enablement, ability, and divine favor. It is God doing something for us or helping us when we do not deserve it. Grace is anointing, God's favor, and the power of the Holy Spirit to meet our weaknesses and inabilities. The apostle James said that God gives us grace and more grace (James 4:6). In other words, He never runs out of grace, but sometimes we stop receiving the grace available to us. We can have all the grace we need, and He will still have more than enough. God wants to help you. Why not let Him do it?

We receive grace through faith, not through fear. We might say faith is our plug-in to the power of God. It is by grace through

> Faith is our plug-in to the power of God.

faith that we are saved (Eph. 2:8), and the same way we are saved is the same way we need to live our daily lives. Faith doesn't buy the blessings of God. Faith is the hand that reaches out and receives what Jesus paid for and offers us graciously.

To help you understand this, think about a lamp. The power the lamp needs in order to work is in the wall socket. The lamp has no power by itself; it only works when it is plugged in. If we try to turn it on before it is plugged in, that does not mean there is a power shortage. It simply means the lamp is not connected. The lamp can provide all the light we need, but it must be plugged in to the power source and turned on.

Are You Unplugged?

The amplification of the word *faith* in Colossians 1:4 is "the leaning of your entire human personality on [God] in absolute trust and confidence in His power, wisdom, and goodness" (AMPC). I love this explanation. It tells me that God is powerful enough to do anything and that He is wise enough to know how to do it and good enough to want to do it even for those who are undeserving. What is our part? We lean on God, rely on Him completely, humble ourselves, ask, and know that apart from Jesus we can do nothing (John 15:5). We are nothing in ourselves, yet we are everything in Christ.

Once you truly see who you are in Christ and recognize the power that is available to you through Him, you will no longer allow fear to rule your life and decisions. I encourage you to start your day with God and realize each morning that you are nothing without God and that it is foolish to merely try to do in your own strength what needs to be done that day. You may push through it, but you won't enjoy it, and you will be exhausted at the end of the day.

God has a better plan. He invites us to enter His rest through placing our faith in Him (Matt. 11:28). The type of rest He offers is not a rest *from* work; it is rest *while* we work.

At one point in the apostle Paul's ministry he said that he worked harder than anybody, but that he was not the one doing the work. The grace of God was working in him and through him. Obviously, Paul made decisions, took action, and didn't allow fear to stop him, but he also knew that nothing he did was possible without God's grace. Paul stayed plugged in. You and I have the same opportunity he had. We can also be sure to keep ourselves connected to God's power.

Short-Circuited Believers

Some people ask for God's power and grace, then lose it or block it. What causes their power to be short-circuited? Think of it this way: When there is a short circuit in a wire, it means that power that should be going into the intended equipment is diverted elsewhere because of a problem in the wiring.

We might also think about this in terms of blowing a fuse or tripping a circuit breaker. I think this happens to some believers. Why? If you lose power in an outlet at home, you may have blown a fuse or tripped a breaker, and the fuse must be replaced or the breaker must be reset before the power will flow again. In our daily lives, if the power flow stops, we may have to make a change because something is hindering its flow. A number of things can cause God's power to short-circuit in our lives. There are a lot more than the three examples that follow, but I think you will get the point with these.

1. Complaining

People may ask for power or grace to accomplish certain difficult tasks. They receive it, and things go along fairly well, but they start to complain about what they have to do in order to complete the task. Grace is intended to show the goodness of God and provoke thanksgiving in the hearts of those who receive it. When that doesn't happen, we can short-circuit God's power. If you want to keep the power flowing, you will need to remain thankful. "Be thankful and say so to Him" (Psalm 100:4 AMPC). A thankful life is a powerful life.

An attitude of gratitude is what I recognized in the woman who had the stroke and preached a message about her good life, even though it is difficult. Although her life is hard and there are many things she cannot do, she is thankful for every single thing she can do. She doesn't have a grumbling attitude, but a thankful one. That keeps the power flow coming into her life. Being thankful is probably one of the most powerful things we can do, and it is so easy to forget to do it.

Paul instructed the believers not to try to do things—even things like growing spiritually—in their own strength, but to let God continually help them. He went on to encourage them to do all things without grumbling, faultfinding, or complaining (Phil. 2:12–14).

The Old Testament book of Daniel tells the story of a young man named Daniel, who had a great deal of power. He had the power not to compromise even when his life was on the line (Dan. 1:8; 6:11–12), and he had the power to allow himself to be thrown into a den of lions, trusting that God would take care of him (Dan. 6:16–23). But Daniel also had a habit of bowing down three times a day and giving thanks to God aloud with his windows open (Dan. 6:10). Even when he was threatened with being eaten by lions, he continued exactly as he had always done and prayed three times a day, giving thanks to God. He didn't cower in fear or give up because of threats. He was a man of faith and a man of gratitude, and those spiritual dynamics empowered him.

2. Feelings of Self-Pity

Feeling sorry for ourselves when we are asked to do difficult things can also short-circuit our ability to receive God's power. We can be powerful or pitiful, but we cannot be both at the same time. Self-pity is like idolatry, because it causes us to turn inward and focus on how we feel and how unfair we think life is to us.

The quality of anyone's life, to a large degree, depends on that person's perspective. For example, two people can face a costly, unexpected repair. One may feel sorry for himself, complain, and become angry, while the other thanks God he has the finances to fix it. Even though both people have the exact same problem, the *problem* does not determine the quality of their lives, their *perspective* does.

Your attitude is yours, and nobody can force you to have a bad attitude about anything if you don't want to have one. Although you may be going through something difficult and seemingly unfair, feeling sorry for yourself will only make it worse. Self-pity leads to discouragement and often to depression. It can also cause people to be jealous and envious of people who don't have the problem they have. Can you be happy for someone who is being blessed while you are suffering?

> Can you be happy for someone who is being blessed while you are suffering?

3. Being Greedy for Glory

Some people receive God's grace (power, favor, help, enablement, ability), and they do great things or they succeed at accomplishing something difficult. At first they are thankful, but after a while, they start taking credit for what God has done.

We have a great example of this in the book of Daniel. The king of Babylon became great due to God's grace, and he regularly gave God the glory and credit for his success. But after a while he built a monument to himself and began boasting about all of his accomplishments. As a result, he lost his kingdom and lived like a wild animal until he finally humbled himself and repented of his sin. Taking the glory that belongs to God will definitely hinder the flow of God's power in our lives.

God spoke through Isaiah that He would not give His glory to another (Isa. 48:11). The apostle Paul said that no mortal man should glory in the presence of God (1 Cor. 1:29). And David said in Psalm 36:11, "Let not the foot of pride overtake me" (AMPC).

When pride chases you, run to God and begin to thank Him for the grace He has given you. Pride will cause believers to short-circuit their power. There are, of course, many other ways to short-circuit our power. Hidden sin of any kind will do it. I strongly recommend that if God is dealing with you about anything, promptly repent and obey Him. God only has your best interest in mind, and, thankfully, His Holy Spirit is in us to help us if we will diligently follow Him.

Stay plugged in to your power source, and you will be amazed at what God can do through you!

PART 2

Confronting Fear

Faith is taking the first step even when you don't see the whole staircase.

Martin Luther King Jr.

When My Fears Took Flight

For years, I allowed fear to get the best of me. I was afraid of something bad happening, afraid of getting hurt, and even afraid to leave my house. But most of all, *I was afraid to fly.*

I flew several times when I was younger. I would be fine for a while, then panic would set in. My eyes would well up with tears, and I would fight to simply catch my breath.

Once I got married and had children, I stopped flying altogether. In my mind, there was too much at stake if something should happen to me. Thankfully, I have a patient husband. To avoid flying, we would take the scenic route and drive thousands of miles on family vacations.

After ten years of this, something inside of me clicked. I thought, *Michele, do you want to keep missing out on things? You can continue to give in to your fears, but what kind of life is that?*

God is my strength, and I could never do anything without Him. But He helped me to realize that He's not going to force me to do anything—I have to take that first step.

I thought, *This first step is going to be a doozy.* We planned the trip, bought the tickets, and, sure enough, the day of departure arrived. I was scared, but this was something I had to do if I wanted to be free.

At the airport, when they called our group to board, I began to panic. Suddenly, the air was sucked out of the room. But I stood up and began walking, step by step, until I was standing on the airplane. I can't say I necessarily enjoyed that first flight, but I knew the worst was over.

Little by little, I also became more confident to try things that I'd always said no to because I was afraid. I still have days when fear tries to stop me. But once I take that first step, it gets much easier—*and my world expands just a little bit more.*

—Michele

CHAPTER 9

Take One Step at a Time

The Lord makes firm the steps of the one who delights in him.

Psalm 37:23

As you're reading this book, you may be thinking of some kind of fear that is hindering you that you would love to conquer. You would love to "do it afraid," but at the same time you may feel overwhelmed even thinking about taking that step. If so, I understand. I felt the same way when God let me know the time was coming when I would need to confront my father about how he had sexually abused me. I was also reluctant when God asked me to quit my job and study for the ministry—even though this was nothing more than a dream in my heart. I could name many other similar situations, so believe me, I understand that fear can be very controlling. The very thought of confronting fear is fearful!

I believe the best way to conquer anything is to take one step at a time without thinking about all the other steps you will need to take later. God gives us His grace one day at a time, and that is because He wants us to trust Him. God's Word teaches us that He delivers us from our enemies little by little (Deut. 7:22). I did not immediately get over being afraid of my father even after I confronted him. But as I persisted for a number of years, doing what

I felt God wanted me to do instead of what fear was telling me, I gained little victories on a regular basis until I could truly say I was almost free. I say "almost" because, you see, I still have one fear that has been around as long as I can remember, and God and I are working together to conquer that one, too.

I understand that most people would like to try to pray away their fear. "God, please deliver me from this fear so I can do what You want me to do," they say. I tried that for years, but God didn't answer that prayer. He answered when I started praying, "God, please give me the courage to face this one day at a time, one step at a time."

Alcoholics Anonymous is well known for their method of teaching alcoholics to face their addiction to alcohol one day at a time. Looking too far down the road is overwhelming, but taking one step at a time, one day at a time, we are able to believe we can do it.

Continue

Our journey with God to freedom in any area must be a lifetime commitment. There is a frequently used word in the Bible that we may overlook, but it is very important and we should pay close attention to it. That word is *continue*. We are told to continue in the Word of God, and then we will know the truth and it will make us free (John 8:31–32 KJV). That freedom doesn't happen magically just because we read the Word, but as we obey it, we are made free. For if we only spend time in the Word occasionally, or when we are in trouble, it won't help us very much.

Freedom is available, but continuing to walk in it will take a commitment of your time to educate yourself about God and His plan for you and to renew your mind. If you wanted to be a doctor, you wouldn't expect to succeed without years of study, and you can think about becoming a victorious Christian in the same way.

As I write this book, I have been a serious student of God's Word for more than forty-three years, and I can say that I am free from many things that once tormented me. I am even free from worrying about things I still need to be set free from because I know I am on a lifetime journey. I can't let up. I can't give up. I can't give in. And I'm always pressing on to the good things that are ahead. In life, we either press forward or we drift backward; we simply cannot remain static.

> I can't let up. I can't give up. I can't give in.

Paul wrote to the Colossians and told them to "be earnest and unwearied and steadfast in your prayer [life], being [both] alert and intent in [your praying] with thanksgiving" (Col. 4:2 AMPC). In his letter to Timothy, his disciple and son in the faith, he wrote, "But as for you, continue in what you have learned and have become convinced of, because you know those from whom you learned it" (2 Tim. 3:14). To the Galatians, he wrote in regard to being enslaved to sin, "It is for freedom that Christ has set us free. Stand firm, then, and do not let yourselves be burdened again by a yoke of slavery" (Gal. 5:1).

Paul was well aware that freedom first had to be gained and then maintained. He knew it was not a onetime event, but a lifetime commitment of continuing to do what was right, day after day after day. Christians today use the word *backslidden* to describe those who have lost a freedom once gained or gone back to a sinful life after having been set free from it. I am not fond of that word, because I don't think we just "slide" into anything. I think we make choices all the time, thousands of them, little choices and big choices. If we continue making the right ones, we will not only gain freedom, but we will keep it.

Every journey begins with one step, and taking one step is all God asks us to do. Take that one step of faith, and then another and another, but think of them one at a time. If you think about how hard your journey will be and how long it may take, you will be defeated before you even begin. Remember, anything you do in obedience to God is something you never have to do alone. He will always be with you, strengthening and encouraging you each step of the way. If you are facing a daunting challenge at this time in your life, fear not, because God is with you.

Getting Started

I knew for many years that if I wanted to enjoy optimum health and longevity, I should be working out, lifting weights, and doing cardio exercises. My writing requires me to sit a lot, and a doctor recently told me that the medical profession now considers a sedentary lifestyle to be the new cancer. He wasn't saying that sitting will cause cancer, but he was trying to impress on me that too much sitting is extremely detrimental to our health.

He gave me an assignment to do while spending lots of time at my computer. He said to stand and move around at least once every forty-five minutes and to do a forty-five-second wall sit! He specifically suggested the wall sits for me because I was having back pain. In case you don't know what a wall sit is, let me just say that it is hard! You back up against a wall and plant your feet and slide about halfway down the wall and stay in that position for forty-five seconds to one minute, or longer if you really want to be in pain. Your quad muscles feel like they are on fire, but that "burn" is supposed to be good for you.

We sit in our automobiles; we sit in front of our computers; we sit while on our phones; we sit and watch television. We sit waiting for appointments, and we sit for many other reasons. I think we can all agree that our lifestyles and society today are always offering us a chair. We ride on escalators and take elevators rather than walking even a single flight of stairs. Most of us are fairly immobile, and then we wonder why, as we age, we begin to feel stiff, have painful joints and no energy, and don't feel well.

For a long time I made excuses for not working out. I didn't see how I could possibly keep any kind of workout schedule with all the traveling I do. Besides that, I am way too busy to go to the gym three days a week. I tried working out a few times at home on my own and always ended up hurting myself, so that became another excuse not to exercise. But then one day I had a thought that I knew was a "God thought." (Although not every thought we have is from God, some are. It is one of the many ways that He speaks to us. This was a God thought for me.) While I was rehearsing my excuses for not working out, suddenly I thought, *Why not just do what you can do when you can do it, and don't worry about what you cannot do? Anything is better than nothing!*

I took a good hard look in the mirror at the condition of my body and could easily see that it had noticeably declined. God let me know that I wouldn't be strong enough for the last third of my journey in ministry if I didn't take some action at that time. It is very important to me to finish what God has assigned me to do, so I got a trainer. My initial plan was to have him teach me some exercises I could do at home and then to see him every couple of months to get new ones. The

> *Do what you can do when you can do it, and don't worry about what you cannot do. Anything is better than nothing!*

amazing thing is that once I got started—once I took that first step—I started seeing such a difference in my body and in my energy level that I wanted to do it more and more. That was in 2005, and I now exercise with a trainer three days a week unless I absolutely cannot do it. We can always find time to do what we truly want to do.

Whatever you are facing, if you will just take that first step, the next one and the one after that won't be so difficult. God shows up when we take action, not when we do nothing.

> God shows up when we take action, not when we do nothing.

Let's say you are afraid of the dark, so you sleep with the lights on even though you are fifty years old. You and your spouse have to sleep in different rooms because they can't sleep with the lights on. You want to turn the lights off, but you have been afraid of the dark since you were a small child. You could begin your journey to freedom by getting into bed and turning the lights off for five minutes. If that is all you can take, turn the lights back on. The next night, leave the lights off for six minutes, and so on. Even if it takes you two years to overcome your fear of the dark, making some progress is better than not making any. If you are happy with your sleeping arrangement, then you don't have to do anything. God loves you just as much if you sleep with the lights on as He does if you sleep in the dark.

I am afraid of snakes, and I don't ever intend to pick one up for even one second or try to work up to playing with them. That is not something I desire to do, and there is no reason for me to do it. Besides, God told Eve in the Garden of Eden that He put enmity between her and the serpent (Gen. 3:15).

I have no interest in skydiving, and if I tried, it would make me afraid. I don't intend to do that, either. But there are many other things I have been afraid of that God let me know I needed to overcome, so I focused on those things.

I had a fear of not pleasing people, and getting over that was vital for me. I was afraid that God wasn't pleased with me, and that also had to go. I was always afraid I wasn't doing enough, so I had to confront that, too. I could share more, but I think you see what I mean.

If some type of fear is holding you back from fulfilling your destiny or from obeying God, don't make excuses for it or simply put up with it for the rest of your life. Take one step to conquer it and then another and another, and don't give up until you arrive at complete freedom, no matter how long it takes. You are never a failure as long as you keep trying.

Inaction breeds doubt and fear. Action breeds confidence and courage. If you want to conquer fear, do not sit home and think about it. Go out and get busy.

Dale Carnegie

Overcoming Doubt

I had been singing professionally for many years and had become very popular. My singing career was my life's dream, and I felt confident that God had called and anointed me to do it. Even the slightest thought that anything could go wrong with my voice was very frightening to me. On one occasion, when I developed laryngitis, the fear I felt was overwhelming.

At the height of my career, I was diagnosed with a cancerous tumor that was very close to my vocal cords. I knew I had to have surgery in order to remove the tumor. There was no chance the operation would not affect my voice. The doctors said they were very sorry, but that my voice would never be the same after surgery.

I tried very hard to have faith in God, but doubt plagued me continually. Finally, I was able to release the entire situation to God. I made up my mind that my joy was in knowing Jesus, not in singing, and I finally cast the care of the outcome of the surgery on Him.

The doctors were right. After the procedure, my voice was not the same. But as I continued healing and took lessons and did exercises to strengthen my vocal cords, my voice returned. It eventually reached the point where it was even better than it had been before!

Through this situation, I learned not to doubt God, but to put Him first in all things and know that He will always do the best for us.

—Cindy

CHAPTER 10

Stand Up to Doubt and Double-Mindedness

He said to them, "Why are you troubled, and why do doubts rise in your minds?"

Luke 24:38

Doubt is nothing more than fear under a different name. I sometimes refer to doubt as "low-level fear," because it is rather subtle. It doesn't manifest the same ways other fears do, but it is nonetheless fear. Perhaps we doubt God by fearing that He will not come through with the help we need or doubt that we can hear from Him and make the right decisions. Maybe we have experienced disappointment with a friend or relative, and now we doubt that we can trust that person. Or, perhaps we have asked God for something and didn't get it, and now we doubt Him. We should realize that if God doesn't give us what we ask for, it's because it would not be the best thing for us.

God wants us to have unshakable trust in Him, but Satan wants our lives to be controlled by a variety of fears manifesting in different ways. Just today, while working on this manuscript on a plane, I realized that we were a little behind schedule, and I might be late for a lunch appointment. I felt fear that my being late might irritate the person waiting for me. It turned out that I was right on time, but those are the kinds of things we need to watch for, because the devil tries to slip fear into our thinking every chance he gets. The point is that I felt fear while writing a book on fear.

If we look at the word *doubt* as it was written in New Testament Greek, it means "to be without a way," or "to be without resources, embarrassed, perplexity, at a loss." *Doubt* can also mean "to stand in two ways" and implies being uncertain about which way to take.

When people are in doubt, they sometimes say, "Everything is just up in the air," which means they don't know what is going to happen and that perhaps things seem confusing and uncertain.

People in this condition would definitely be double-minded. They decide to do one thing and then begin to doubt their decision, so they decide to do something else. Then, they feel unsure of that, so they may go back to their original decision. This can go on until they become so confused that they may give up and make no decision at all.

If we truly want to live free from fear, we must learn to live without doubt. To live boldly, we must walk in faith. The devil sends doubt into our lives to war against our faith. I don't know how you feel about it, but I hate being full of doubt and feeling unable to make a decision.

Abraham had a promise from God that he and his wife would have a child even though, from a natural perspective, they were too old to do so (Gen. 18:11). They needed a miracle, and they waited on God, but the fulfillment of the promise was slow in coming. Paul wrote that while Abraham waited, "No unbelief or distrust made him waver (doubtingly question) concerning the promise of God, but he grew strong and was empowered by faith as he gave praise and glory to God" (Rom. 4:20 AMPC).

Jairus had opportunity to doubt while he waited for Jesus to come and heal his daughter, who was at the point of death (Mark 5:22–23). Jesus had said He would come and heal her, but along the way He was interrupted by a woman who needed help, and He stopped to help her. I can easily imagine that the waiting father was feeling impatient and wanted Jesus to hurry. Perhaps he doubted whether or not Jesus would arrive on time to save her. While Jairus was waiting for Jesus, one of his servants came and told him that his daughter had died. Jesus overheard the report and said, "Don't be afraid; just believe" (Mark 5:36). That sounds simple enough, but when you are the one with the pressing problem, it is more difficult than it sounds.

How often do you let doubt steal your faith? Sometimes it happens so fast we don't even recognize that the devil has stolen an opportunity for something good to happen. All of us have attacks of doubt launched against us, so don't feel condemned if it happens to you. The key is to recognize it, resist it, and be like Abraham and let no doubt or unbelief make you waver concerning your faith in God.

> How often do you let doubt steal your faith?

It is easy to justify our doubts. Satan will help us to be indecisive and uncertain about a lot of things and give us good reasons for the doubt we experience. God says He is able to do exceedingly and abundantly, above all we can ask or think (Eph. 3:20), but we do need to ask in faith.

> But when you ask, you must believe and not doubt, because the one who doubts is like a wave of the sea, blown and tossed by the wind. That person should not expect to

receive anything from the Lord. Such a person is double-minded and unstable in all they do.

James 1:6–8

Self-Doubt

Self-doubt is one of our biggest problems. I believe we doubt ourselves more than we doubt God. Most of us are pretty sure all things are possible with God, but we doubt He will do the impossible for us. We doubt whether or not we can hear from God. We doubt we are making the right decisions, and this can be tormenting because every day is filled with decisions that need to be made. Some are small and rather minor, but others can be life-altering.

Sometimes the only way to find out if we are right about something is to be willing to take a chance on being wrong. It's amazing—even if we do make a mistake, God can take it and work good from it (Rom. 8:28). I believe that a large part of what we learn in life is learned from our mistakes.

The only way to learn how to hear from God is through practice. We learn through God's Word and our life experience. I still study how to hear from God often, and I usually buy any new book I see that is about hearing from Him and is based on Scripture. I've learned a lot about hearing God's voice, but I want to keep my faith strong in this area, and the way to do that is to study and read regularly.

> I believe that a large part of what we learn in life is learned from our mistakes.

Do you often think:

I shouldn't have done that!
I shouldn't have said that!

I shouldn't have bought that!
I shouldn't have gone there!
I shouldn't have eaten that!
I didn't pray long enough or the right way!
I spent too much at the grocery store!
I talk too much!
I should be quieter!
I should have spoken up!
I should be a better parent!
I have trouble making decisions!

If you ever want to make good decisions, stop saying you have trouble doing it. Start declaring that you believe you hear God's voice clearly and that you are able to make good decisions.

It is a miserable tyranny to think excessively about the things we should have done or shouldn't have done but can't do anything about now. Satan loves to wait until we have made a mistake and then remind us of it over and over. But God gives us an inner caution or a lack of peace when we are headed in the wrong direction before we make a mistake. But if, while thinking we are doing the right thing, it ends up being wrong, God still loves us just as much as He always has. And if we need help, He will help us.

> If, while thinking we are doing the right thing, it ends up being wrong, God still loves us just as much as He always has. And if we need help, He will help us.

If you want to hear from God and be led by the Holy Spirit, you begin by believing you can and do hear from God. Then be willing to surrender your will to His, and continue in faith with thanksgiving while you're waiting for your breakthrough. After He prayed, Jesus said, "Father, I thank you that you have heard me" (John

11:41). He didn't doubt or wonder whether or not His Father heard Him. He thanked Him that He heard Him. I recommend doing the same thing after you pray; let the confession that God hears you and that you can hear from Him build faith in your heart.

When Jesus said, "Father, I thank you that you have heard me," is it possible He was making a verbal confession of faith to drown out the lies of Satan (who was probably telling Him that God didn't hear Him)? I think it is possible, because as our High Priest, Jesus went through all of the same things we do. The writer of Hebrews said that Jesus has "a shared feeling with our weaknesses and infirmities," and He understands how we feel because He "has been tempted in every respect as we are" (Heb. 4:15 AMPC). In other words, He has gone through the same things and been attacked by the devil in the same ways we are.

Fear is a formidable enemy no matter how it presents itself, but with God's help we can and will recognize the devil's lies and keep going forward in our walk with Him. While it is true that we are in a spiritual battle, according to God's Word, we already have the victory and are simply walking it out in our daily lives. So another good truth to declare is "I have the victory."

Perhaps you have never thought about doubt as a form of fear, but that is exactly what it is, and it is something that needs to be confronted. It's fine to ask God to show you if you are headed in a wrong direction or have made a bad decision, but don't be afraid that you are *always* wrong about your decisions. God has given us free will, which means that although He wants to be involved in everything we do, He still wants us to think, plan, use wisdom, and make choices. There are many times when God has no particular desire for us to do one thing or another. He gives us freedom to choose as long as our choice is in line with His Word. One father gave a good example of this. He said that when

he tells his son and daughter to go and play, he has no prefer-
ence whether they play in their rooms or outside in the backyard.
They can play with their toys or play a game. He just wants them
to play. How they go about it is up to them. Can you imagine
small children being told to go play
and then being fearful that they are
playing the wrong way? God tells
us to come to Him as little children (Matt. 18:3), and that means
to approach Him with a trusting
attitude.

> Can you imagine small
> children being told to go play
> and then being fearful that
> they are playing the wrong
> way?

The Fear of Being Wrong

The fear of being wrong is the root of self-doubt and double-
mindedness, but if we will realize that making wrong decisions
doesn't make us wrong as people, we can avoid a lot of misery.
God loves us whether all of our decisions are right or not, so we
don't need to fear being wrong. People who do great things usually fail at what they are trying to do the first several tries, but
they don't believe they are failures. They simply know that they
tried something and it didn't work.

When I am recording television shows, if I make a mistake
(and I do), my producers tell me, "Don't worry about it, because
we can fix it in post." What do they mean? They mean that they
can fix it by removing it through editing procedures before it
goes on television for everyone to see. I think God can also fix
our mistakes "in post" (after they have been made), and I am sure
He has all the editing equipment He needs to take our mistakes
and make something good from them. When you think you may

have made a mistake, just ask God to take it and make it work out for good (Rom. 8:28).

Another good way to handle a mistake is to simply admit it and go on to the next challenge in life. I have found that people respect me more if I admit my mistakes instead of trying to cover them up or make excuses for them.

You can look at being wrong in a more positive way and lose the fear of it. Everyone makes mistakes, so do the best you can and trust God to teach you as you journey through life.

> *I have found that people respect me more if I admit my mistakes instead of trying to cover them up or make excuses for them.*

When you need to make a decision, pray about it, think over your options, consider the pros and cons of each way you could go, and then boldly make a decision. You may be wrong sometimes, but you will be right more than you will be wrong because you are wiser than you think you are. You have the mind of Christ, and His Spirit dwells in you (1 Cor. 2:16; John 14:17). Every day when you get out of bed, you already have an advantage because God is with you.

God is for you, so it really doesn't matter who is against you or what people think (Rom. 8:31). Live boldly for God, and enjoy the life He has given you. Don't let doubt and double-mindedness steal your peace and joy.

Gratitude looks to the past and love to the present; fear, avarice, lust, and ambition look ahead.

C. S. Lewis, *The Screwtape Letters*

Tumbling through My Fear

When I was eleven years old and in fifth grade, we received notice at school that junior high cheerleading tryouts would be held soon. I had waited for this day for a long time. I had worked very hard on my tumbling in order to be ready for tryouts, but I wasn't sure what else to expect or what was required.

The first day of tryouts is when the fear hit. I found out that I would be competing not only against ten or fifteen girls from my class, but also against sixth- and seventh-grade girls who had already been on the team. I also quickly learned that the tumbling mats weren't the same as I was used to, and that no one would help me if I had trouble with my tumbling.

The coach needed to evaluate our skills but told us that if we couldn't do any tumbling, we should just stay seated. So, I stayed on the bleachers. When my dad picked me up afterward, I got in the car and started to cry. He asked me what was wrong, and I said, "I didn't do my tumbling. I was too afraid of falling and hurting myself." He encouraged me and reminded me that I had two more nights to do it, but he said we needed to pray against the fear. He asked me if that was all I was worried about, and I said, "I was also afraid of being embarrassed if I fell in front of the older girls and the coach." He told me, "Sometimes, we have to do things afraid!" We prayed on the way home, and I started to feel better, but I was still nervous.

The next night when my dad picked me up from tryouts, I came running out and jumped into his arms and hugged him tight. He asked me what this was about, and I said, "I did it! I did it afraid, just like you said, and just like we prayed. And, I did it really well!"

I made the team, but the most important lesson I learned was that sometimes you just have to do it afraid!

—Sophie

CHAPTER 11

Refuse to Regret the Past or Dread the Future

Let your eyes look straight ahead; fix your gaze directly before you.

Proverbs 4:25

When Moses asked God what His name was, God replied, "I AM WHO I AM" (Exod. 3:14). When the disciples were in a boat with Jesus during a severe storm they were greatly afraid. Jesus responded to their fear saying, "Take courage! I AM! Stop being afraid!" (Matt. 14:27 AMPC).

God is present in the moment. He is present today. He does not refer to Himself as "I was," or "I will be," but as "I AM." He is omnipresent, which means He is present all the time, everywhere. If we live in the regrets of the past or in dread of the future, we miss what He has for us today. The greatest moment in your life is the present one. Live it fully by being present in the present.

> The greatest moment in your life is the present one.

We have all made mistakes in the past, and we will all make more mistakes in the future. We have all endured injustices in the past, and more than likely we will experience them at some time in the future, but to spend today worrying and fretting about them is a waste of time. Today we can ask God to take our past and redeem it, or we might say "recycle" it and turn it into something good. People have come up with all kinds of ways to recycle pieces of trash and turn them into things that are usable. The creators of that idea probably admire themselves for being so creative, but God has been recycling trash since time began. He takes the broken pieces of our hearts and lives and recycles them into something useful.

The apostle Paul said that God chooses the foolish, the weak, and what is low and despised by the world to be used in His Kingdom. He does this so no human being can boast in His presence (1 Cor. 1:26–31).

By the time I became a young adult, I was broken in every way. My heart was broken, my soul was wounded, I had a very poor self-image, and I had no true confidence. Something in me, which I now know was God, whispered to my soul that I could do something great, but it seemed so impossible that my mind warred against any such thought. In addition, Satan continually planted in my mind false thoughts that I was trash and useless. He told me I would always have to settle for second-rate everything because I was damaged from the abuse I had endured.

Thankfully, the more I got to know God through His Word, and the more I watched Him work in my life, the more I realized that Satan is a liar and that I didn't have to base my present life on my past. The same is true for you. Your history is not your destiny. As this verse indicates, God is clear about the need to let go of the past and enjoy the life He has for you now:

Forget the former things; do not dwell on the past. See,
I am doing a new thing! Now it springs up; do you not

perceive it? I am making a way in the wilderness and
streams in the wasteland.

Isaiah 43:18–19

I still remember how joyful this Scripture passage made me
when I first learned of it. It is full of hope for anyone who needs a
new beginning. God's promise is that when we receive Christ and
live in Him, old things pass away and all things become brand-
new (2 Cor. 5:17). Living in the regrets of yesterday indicates that
we don't believe God is big enough to take care of our past and
give us a fresh start, but He is. I can't resist the opportunity to
share with you a few scriptures that include this promise:

> Because of the Lord's great love we are not consumed, for
> his compassions never fail. They are new every morning;
> great is your faithfulness.
>
> Lamentations 3:22–23

> But one thing I do: Forgetting what is behind and
> straining toward what is ahead, I press on toward the goal
> to win the prize for which God has called me heavenward
> in Christ Jesus.
>
> Philippians 3:13–14

> See, I will create new heavens and a new earth. The
> former things will not be remembered, nor will they come
> to mind.
>
> Isaiah 65:17

Everything in our lives does not instantly change when we
receive Christ. We don't look different, nor do all of our circum-

stances immediately improve, but the possibility of change is now our promise from God. I like to say that He makes us new spiritual clay, and if we will allow Him to, He will mold us into His image (Rom. 8:29). Just imagine what a major change that is. To be changed from what we once were to how Jesus is—now that is quite an amazing transformation.

The Power of Hope

God desires for us to live filled with hope, and that is very difficult to do if we are simultaneously living with regrets about the past or dreading the future. Hope is a positive expectation that something good is going to happen to us. The apostle Peter said that we are born again into a living hope (1 Pet. 1:3). Robert Schuller said, "Let your hopes, not your hurts, shape your future."

I had a disappointing life until I was in my early thirties. I had experienced a lot of pain and injustice, to the point that I was afraid of hoping for anything better, fearing that I would only be disappointed when it did not happen. "Why bother?" I asked myself. I let my regrets from the past not only ruin my present but also cast a dark shadow on what I perceived my future would be. But, my experience with God and the promises in His Word have changed my expectations. Now I have hope! I often say, "I didn't have a good beginning in life, but I fully intend to have a great finish." The same is true for you.

> I didn't have a good beginning in life, but I fully intend to have a great finish.

A good biblical example is that of Saul. He was Israel's first king, and although God anointed him for that position, he was rebellious. At one point, God told the prophet Samuel that he regretted making Saul the king of Israel. Samuel was grieved and cried out to the Lord all night (1 Sam. 15:10–11). Although I am sure God was disappointed, He told Samuel to stop grieving over Saul and to go and anoint a king to take his place (1 Sam. 16:1). I have always enjoyed the message these scriptures bring because they give us a pattern for the attitude we should have toward things that don't turn out as we had hoped. We should repent and grieve our failure or disappointment, but then go on to something new. Although people fail, God is never without a plan.

There is nothing you have done nor is there anything that has been done to you for which God doesn't have a remedy. I urge you not to let the devil rob you of hope any longer. Hope is a great motivator. It gives you a reason to get out of bed each morning, trusting that you serve a good God who has a good plan for your life.

In December 2017 I was suddenly afflicted with a debilitating illness. I had previously been very strong and had a lot of endurance, but suddenly I was unable to do much because I had absolutely no energy. Being a woman who believes in the power of prayer, I prayed daily—often many times a day—for God's healing or for answers to my problem. The medical profession offered a little help. They said I had adrenal exhaustion from the stress of working too hard for too long. A doctor I trusted and had known for a long time told me that I had to rest externally and internally for one year to eighteen months, and that I would probably never be able to work as hard as I previously had. This was all very hard on me emotionally, because I didn't want to rest for eighteen months, but I actually felt so bad I didn't have much choice.

I clearly needed God to move on my behalf. I had commitments to fulfill, and God was faithful to give me the energy I needed to do what I absolutely had to do, but I was faced with making some big changes in my lifestyle. Many people prayed, and I did my best to keep a good attitude, believing each day that I would see a difference. Day after day, I stayed the same. At times that was discouraging, but I knew I had to have hope. After almost eighteen months, for no apparent reason, I began to feel stronger. At first it was a few days here and there, and it took time, but over the next few months I felt good again and had the stamina to do all I needed to do. Why did it take eighteen months? Why weren't my prayers answered sooner? I don't know why. "Why?" is the question we never stop asking, but we rarely get an answer. Trust always requires unanswered questions.

I learned from this experience that no matter how long it takes for God to answer, we should never give up. While we wait for our complete breakthrough, God gives us strength to keep going. Let this story encourage you not to let anything steal your hope. Make hope a habit, and I believe you will be released from the fear that things will never get better in your life.

God is "I Am." He is able to do all things, and His desire is for you to live in the present, not the past or the future. When I became sick, I regretted not taking better care of myself before I was forced to do so. But I knew that carrying regret would add more stress, so I repented and asked God to teach me and heal me.

Don't miss what God has for you today by living in regret. Today is an important day in your life. It is actually the most important day of your life, because right at this moment it is the only day you are assured of, so live it fully and trust God to take care of your past and your future.

Defeating Dread

Everyone makes mistakes. Whether you are dealing with mistakes from many years ago or mistakes from five minutes ago, the past is behind you. Don't waste the moment you are living in right now in regret, fear of the future, guilt, bitterness, an unforgiving attitude, or any other negative and useless emotion that has the power to steal this day. As I wrote in chapter 1, you can choose how you want your life to be, so make a choice that will open the door for God to intervene in your affairs.

As I have mentioned, dread is a type of fear. Dread is the fear that you won't be able to do what you need to do, or that you won't be able to enjoy yourself while you are doing it. It is looking into the unknown and feeling panic because you don't see a nice blueprint laid out in front of you that shows you exactly what the future holds. If God wrote mystery books, each of our lives would be a book in itself. God has promised to take care of us, but He has not given us the details of how or when He will do it.

> *If God wrote mystery books, each of our lives would be a book in itself.*

We can dread anything from retirement to doing the dishes, but any form of dread drains us of much-needed energy. Even when we dread simple things, such as going to the grocery store or driving to work in rush hour traffic, what we are really doing is deciding ahead of time that we cannot do those things and enjoy them. But the truth is that we can enjoy all things if we do them with God and for His glory.

You can decide, for example, that you are going to clean your home because you want God to be pleased that you are taking good care of what He has given you. Or you can dread doing it, verbalizing often how much you dread it. Sure enough, when the time comes to clean, you will have a bad attitude the entire time you are doing what needs to be done. Anything you have to do, you may as well do it with a good attitude, because having a bad attitude won't release you from the responsibility of doing it.

As I mentioned earlier, I have been working out with a trainer three times a week for more than fourteen years. I often feel dread trying to get stirred up in my mind when I think about working out, but I have learned that if I am going to do it anyway, I may as well enjoy it.

Anytime you start to dread anything, pray immediately for God to give you the grace to do what you need to do with a good attitude. God answers prayers, but He cannot answer a prayer you don't pray. Ask for God's help in everything you do, and you will find it much easier.

God told the Israelites to not dread or be afraid of their enemies (Deut. 20:1). Jesus said that the thief comes only to "steal and kill and destroy," but that He came so we might "have and enjoy" our lives (John 10:10 AMPC). How can we enjoy life if we dread the things that life requires us to do? Consider this scripture:

> Whatever you do, work at it with all your heart, as working for the Lord, not for human masters.
>
> Colossians 3:23

We can't work heartily if we dread the work we need to do. Satan comes up with all kinds of ways to keep us from enjoying our daily lives. Many of them are subtle, and we would never recognize them if God didn't reveal them to us. I spent a lot of years in either regret or dread until God opened my eyes to see that by doing so, I was missing today. He is "I Am," and that means He is present right now. If we want to enjoy and benefit from living in His presence, we need to focus on today, not yesterday or tomorrow.

Naturally, we all make some plans for the future, and Proverbs encourages us to be good stewards and to plan wisely (Prov. 16:9; 27:23), but that is totally different from looking at the future with fear and dread. Have a wise financial plan for retirement, but don't worry about it. Save now for your children's college and wedding expenses, but don't worry about them.

If you want to be happy, don't dwell on the past or worry about the future. Focus on living fully in the present. Don't set aside your happiness or put it off until sometime in the future.

Medical experts are discovering the value of living today and focusing on what we are doing now. They refer to it as practicing mindfulness. What they have discovered is not anything new, because Solomon talked about it in Ecclesiastes. Ecclesiastes 5:1 says, "Give your mind to what you are doing" (AMPC). This is something I have not been very good at, because I am usually doing one thing while thinking about the next thing I am going to do, but I am praying about that, and God is helping me. Some habits are hard to break, but if we keep at it, with God's help, we can change.

Make today count. It is the day the Lord has made, and we should rejoice and be glad in it (Ps. 118:24).

One of the greatest discoveries a man makes, one of his great surprises, is to find he can do what he was afraid he couldn't do.

Henry Ford

Conquering the Fear of Being Alone

Ever since I was young, I've had this terrible fear of being alone. Not wanting to go in the basement alone. Not wanting to carry a basket of clothes upstairs by myself. Not wanting to stay home alone for just five minutes while my mom ran across the street to the neighbors—even at a reasonable age of twelve, I might add. This was all out of fear that something would scare me, that something would happen to me, that I wouldn't be protected.

While I believe it started from sneaking a peek of a scary ghost movie when I was eight years old, this fear only became more rooted as I hid under the covering of family and friends, pleading with someone to always go with me, always do things with me, always be with me.

Fast-forward to my twenties, and as much as I thought I simply preferred to be with someone, I realized I had a deeply rooted fear I needed to give to God. I realized how much I relied on others and wanted to go from family to roommates to a husband so I'd never have to be alone.

If I was by myself, did it mean I'd be targeted and something bad would happen to me? If I was alone, did it mean I wasn't loved and no one wanted to be with me? This fear brought me to the point of shaking and losing sleep.

As soon as I recognized the fear for what it was, opportunities came left and right for me to step out, be brave, and do things alone. All of them probably came my way before, but I managed to always have someone or *make* someone be with me. The greatest opportunity, I believe, was God calling me to move to an entirely different state, away from all my family and friends, not knowing a single person. I had to trust Him with every bit of my being.

Over the course of six and a half years, I had to show up for classes and make new friends without being introduced by someone familiar. I had to go to the grocery store, doctor's appointments, and the car repair shop by myself. I even had to celebrate Thanksgiving one year and New Year's the next all alone—not because I wasn't loved or didn't have invitations, but because God was trying to teach me something.

Little by little, I've been conquering this fear. It's not gone completely, but I can confidently say that had I not given it to God and seen it for what it was, I wouldn't have been able to live the past sixteen months in my own apartment. Alone.

—Megan

CHAPTER 12

Take Courage and Be Strong

But the people, the men of Israel, took courage and strengthened themselves and again set their battle line in the same place where they formed it the first day.

Judges 20:22 AMPC

God offers us courage, and Satan offers us fear; the choice is ours to make. I am struck by the statement that the men of Israel "took courage." It makes me think that courage must always be available, but we have to take it if we want it to do us any good. When we choose courage, fear has no place in which to take up residence in us.

We usually focus on trying to get rid of a problem, but I believe we should focus more on receiving the answer to the problem. I wrote a book titled *Making Good Habits, Breaking Bad Habits*. The teaching in it is, I believe, a little unusual because it urges people to focus on developing good habits that will automatically get rid of bad ones. For example, if I need to lose weight and I focus constantly on what I *can't* eat, that will only make me want to eat bad foods more. But if I focus on all the healthy foods I *can* eat, then I will make better choices and ultimately lose weight.

If I focus on my faults all of the time, they will most likely increase, but if I focus on how far God has brought me and how much He has already changed me, then I have confidence that He will do even more and more.

What we focus on is what develops in our lives. If I want a picture of Dave, but I focus my camera lens on a tree, I will get a picture of a tree rather than one of him. Try focusing on being courageous rather than not being afraid, and I believe you will find yourself being more bold and courageous than ever before. It may take time to train your mind to think differently, but it will be worth it in the end. Don't defeat yourself by exerting energy doing the wrong thing, which will never get you the right result. Fighting with fear will strengthen it instead of getting rid of it. The best thing to do is confront it with courage and do what fear tells you not to do.

Don't just pray for fear to go away. Instead pray for God to fill you with boldness, courage, and confidence. Our wrong thinking often defeats us, but since wrong thinking can defeat us, then right thinking can help us. Romans 12:2 indicates that we will never experience the good life God has for us unless our minds are completely renewed by God's Word.

> *Don't just pray for fear to go away. Instead pray for God to fill you with boldness, courage, and confidence.*

In the early years of my walk with God, I spent a lot of time and effort trying to get things God had already given me. I just didn't know at the time that they already belonged to me in Him, through my relationship with Christ. He gave them freely by His grace, but since I didn't realize that, I kept trying to get what I already had. I tried to earn God's love, but He loved me while I was still in sin (Rom. 5:8). I tried to be right with God by doing everything right, and each day I was disappointed in myself because no matter how much I did right, I always did something wrong. Then I learned that I was already right with God because Jesus took all my sin and gave me His right standing with God (2 Cor. 5:21). I learned countless other lessons that set me free from trying to get what I already had.

God commissioned Joshua to lead the Israelites across the Jordan River into the Promised Land. In Joshua 1:9, He said to Joshua, "Be strong and courageous. Do not be afraid." Notice that God first said to "be strong and courageous," and after that "do not be afraid."

I think we can experience fear and courage at the same time, and whichever is the strongest is the one that will rule. I am sure Esther felt fear when God called her to save her people by asking the king to help her, but she fasted and prayed and ended up with the courage to do as God asked her to do (Esther 4:16–5:3). Her courage was greater than her fear. Feelings of fear may never completely go away, but if we regularly seek God for courage, we will always be strong enough to do whatever we need to do. We will just do it afraid! Courage confronts the fear and moves beyond it.

Encouragement

It seems that in order to have courage, we often need a lot of encouragement. Moses had spoken to Joshua the same words God spoke to him later, so he must have needed to hear them more than once.

> Be strong and courageous. Do not be afraid or terrified because of them, for the Lord your God goes with you; he will never leave you nor forsake you.
>
> Deuteronomy 31:6

Moses encouraged Joshua. A short while later, God encouraged Joshua, too. Satan wants to "*discourage*" us. In other words, he wants to block or hinder the courage God has for us. God didn't create us to be fearful, and He does not give us a spirit of fear. He gives us boldness, faith, courage, and confidence, but we have to use them. The more we use what God has given us, the stronger it becomes.

Joshua had to be bold and courageous many, many times as he led the people through the Promised Land, because everywhere they went they had to conquer enemies in order to possess the land. You may feel that you are continually facing one problem after another, but you should also know and stay aware of the fact that God is with you and will always lead you to victory if you follow Him. I'm sure you might feel like there is no end in sight to your struggles, but God knows there is and exactly when it will be.

You are God's child, and you are precious to Him. Paul taught us that we have not received a spirit of slavery to put us in bondage to fear, but we "have received the Spirit of adoption" by "which we cry, Abba (Father)!" (Rom. 8:15 AMPC). *Abba* is an intimate word that is equivalent to the English word *Daddy*. We have been brought near to God by the blood of Jesus Christ (Eph. 2:13) and are joint heirs with Him. God has adopted us and given us full rights as His sons and daughters (Rom. 8:15–17; 2 Cor. 6:18).

Rather than focusing on all the bad things we can be afraid of, let's focus on who our Father is and remember that with Him by our side, there is nothing to fear.

I believe God has given each of us the ministry of encouragement. The Holy Spirit is an encourager. He lives in us to help and encourage us, and He wants to work through each of us to encourage others. Let's help people believe they can do all things through Christ instead of joining with Satan to discourage them. None of us would willingly let Satan work through us, but he often does. He puts thoughts, imaginations, and attitudes in our minds about people's abilities and decisions, and unless we are thoroughly committed to never discouraging anyone, we will express those thoughts and never realize the devil is using us to discourage people. Our words contain power. Proverbs 18:21 tells us they hold the power of life and death, so we should choose to speak only life-giving words.

When I stepped out into ministry, plenty of people discouraged me and told me that I couldn't and shouldn't do it, but God gave me courage. He personally encouraged me, and He also put a few people in my life who affirmed me. They were for me and wanted to see me succeed, and their support was a great motivator for me. It kept me going through the really rough times when it seemed that those who had discouraged me were right after all. Encouragement is a very important ministry and one we should engage in often. Uplifting others comes naturally to some people. But that is not the case with everyone, and those of us who are not naturally inclined in that direction will need to be purposefully encouraging. My first impulse would be to see what is wrong with a person or thing, but God has taught me that my first impulse usually comes from my flesh, and I need to make sure my impulses agree with His Word before I act on them.

God has taught me that my first impulse usually comes from my flesh, and I need to make sure my impulses agree with His Word before I act on them.

The apostle Paul included instruction about being encouraging to others in many of his teachings. This is one of my favorites:

And we urge you, brothers and sisters, warn those who are idle and disruptive, encourage the disheartened, help the weak, be patient with everyone.

1 Thessalonians 5:14

There are times when we need to admonish (warn or reprimand) others, but we are also to encourage the fainthearted (fearful) and weak (Isa. 35:3–4). It is amazing how much strength we can gain from encouragement we receive at just the right time. Not long ago someone sent me a text that simply said, "God wants you to be encouraged that you are in the right place at the right time." Over the next few days I reread that text several times. We had recently made some changes in my schedule, and those reassuring words gave me strength to believe we had done the right thing. Having that confirmation that I was right where I was supposed to be was comforting and gave me confidence.

We may think of something we should or could say to another person that sounds quite normal to us, but it could be almost miraculous for them. One thing is for sure: You can never do the wrong thing when you sincerely encourage other people.

Meditate and Declare

God's Word teaches us to meditate on it. Just as we have to chew our food well to release the nutrition in it, we need to meditate on God's Word to get the most out of it. To meditate simply means to roll over and over in your mind or to think about something often.

Keep this Book of the Law always on your lips; meditate on it day and night, so that you may be careful to do everything written in it. Then you will be prosperous and successful.

Joshua 1:8

God gave this instruction to Joshua and the Israelites as they were preparing to go into the Promised Land. He was telling them to declare His Word out of their mouths and to think about it. Doing so would give them the ability to be obedient to it. Please don't rush past this very important truth. Meditating on and declaring God's Word is one of the most important things you can do, and it will ultimately help you more than you can imagine.

Here is an example of something you can declare and think about every day:

> I am a child of God and He loves me. He is always with me, and therefore I will not fear. I can do all things through Christ, who is my strength. When I feel weak, He encourages me to keep pressing on. I am bold, courageous, and confident in Christ. No weapon formed against me shall prosper because greater is He who is in me than he who is in the world.

This declaration is composed of portions of several scriptures and is an effective way to meditate on them. If you declare this twice a day for thirty days, you will find yourself feeling much better about yourself and your abilities.

Mark 4:24 teaches us to be careful about what we hear and says that the measure of thought and study we give to the truth we hear is the measure of virtue and knowledge that will come back to us. In other words, the more we declare and meditate on the Word we hear or read, the more it will mean to us and the more it will produce good fruit in our lives. Just because we hear something does not mean we have learned it. Hearing and knowing are two different things. People can go to church every Sunday for ten years, and although they have heard the Word over and over, they still live as though they know nothing about it. That is probably because what they received as information never became revelation to them through further thought and study.

Our ministers cannot help us become spiritually strong unless we cooperate and do our part. You might consider writing down the reference for every scripture you hear when someone is teaching God's Word. Then, in your own study time, you can look up each one, read it aloud, and think about what it really means to you personally. Some people think all they need to do is go to church, but if all they do is just sit there, it will never make them strong Christians, just as sitting in a garage all day won't make them a car.

Every time you meditate on being courageous, you are defeating fear. I want to remind you again not to simply pray for God to deliver you from fear, but pray for Him to give you amazing courage and confidence.

Courage Takes a Chance

Courage is courageous, meaning that it takes a chance and tries to do something rather than sitting idly by and doing nothing. We often say, "Somebody needs to do something about that," but what if

> *Doing nothing produces nothing.*

we are the ones who need to do something? Doing nothing produces nothing.

There are times when a fine line exists between being courageous and being foolish, so use wisdom, but don't shrink back in fear. Don't be afraid to take a chance. You have to step out to find out whether you can do something or not. Don't let the fear of failure keep you from trying.

I believe there are times when we think too long about something we feel we should do and talk ourselves out of taking action before we even try. Peter asked Jesus to bid him to come out of the boat and walk on the water. He then climbed out of the boat and walked on water with Jesus for a short period of time, but then he started looking at and thinking about the storm and began to sink (Matt. 14:28–31). It is almost as if he took a leap of faith when Jesus said, "Come," and then started thinking about what he was doing, and that opened a door for fear to defeat him.

I function more by instinct than I do by excessive thinking. Naturally, I think about things before doing them, but if I sense in my heart I can do something and that God wants me to do it, I quickly take action, because I know the devil will do his best to prevent me from doing anything that is good or helpful. I will admit there have been times when I should have given more thought to things and that doing so could have spared me a problem. But being a person of action has produced many more benefits than problems in my life.

I sometimes ask for advice or check to see what someone else thinks about what I am going to do, but I am not the kind of person who needs several people to approve before I will take action. Sometimes, when we start getting too many people's opinions, we end up confused, because most of the time everyone we talk to has a different opinion.

I realize we are all different, and you may not be like me. Maybe you need more time to think, and if so, that is fine. But

I encourage you not to think about what could possibly go wrong so much that you talk yourself out of what you think you should do.

God's usual way of leading us is either by His Word or by discernment (the leading of the Holy Spirit). Discernment is a deep knowing that may sometimes conflict with our natural thinking. There have been times when, for no apparent reason, I felt strongly that someone working with us would end up being a problem. But in an effort not to be judgmental or suspicious, I kept that person on our staff. Sure enough, they eventually caused trouble through stirring up strife or, in one instance, stealing from us. It is much wiser to trust your heart (your spirit) than it is to trust your feelings or natural thoughts.

Have you ever asked someone a question and they quickly said, "Well, off the top of my head, I think..." and then they told you what they thought? Frankly, the last place we should get advice from is the top of our own head or anyone else's. We want the right answer, which usually takes going a bit deeper than the top of our head.

As we close this chapter, let me remind you once more that courage is stronger than fear. The answer to fear is always the same: "Be strong and courageous, for God is with you."

Each time we face our fears, we gain strength, courage, and confidence in the doing.

Theodore Roosevelt

Overcoming Insecurity

I am afraid to be vulnerable. Is it a bit ironic to be open about vulnerability? Admitting the fear is no hurdle. It's those moments when I actually need to be vulnerable that are the challenge. Your typical phobias like snakes, spiders, cockroaches, drowning, and heights give me no fright.

I am not a shy girl—quite the opposite. I'm outgoing, very conversational (chatty), independent, and adventurous, and I'm from a family of eight siblings with inherent Pollyanna-like optimism. I'll boldly interject in the right circumstances and am willing to candidly discuss almost anything, at length.

What makes me hold an anxious breath and squirm in my seat are matters of the heart—such as love, trust, intimacy, and deeper relationships—where my issues, past mistakes, character flaws, and failures are exposed. Old insecurities and out-of-balance emotions well up inside of me, and I start to react to them physically. My heart rate increases, I fidget more than normal, I get a little nauseous, and I have even had the hair on the back of my neck stand up.

Then my mind begins to race. I second-guess revealing more of myself. I think about what I have already shared and wonder if it should be kept secret. Can I trust it was received respectfully and without rejection? Is it all the other person will see when they look at me from now on? In the wake of those questions I decide to distance myself, because I realize that my vulnerability has made me defenseless if the other person should want to attack or hurt me in some way.

Funny, I gravitate toward transparent people. I admire how they can admit their failed goals or broken hearts, how their weakness got the better of them again, billboarding their imperfections for any and all oncoming traffic. I observe in awe how they have no sense of restraint. I feel special and trusted when a friend shares something private with me. I get a sense of joy and honor that I'm there for that person.

"And they overcame him by the blood of the Lamb and by the word of their testimony" (Rev. 12:11 NKJV). God's Word is power. His Word is healing. His Word brings security and confidence. I choose God's Word over my fear. I will face the fear with God's courage and be vulnerable, even when I'm afraid.

—Autumn

CHAPTER 13

Learn to Be Secure and Confident

You will be secure, because there is hope; you will look about you and take your rest in safety. You will lie down, with no one to make you afraid.

Job 11:18–19

Feeling insecure and lacking confidence are symptoms of fear, and their source is the devil. It stands to reason that people won't accomplish much in life if they are afflicted with these two problems. God offers us security in Him and confidence in Him, but of course, the devil wants to steal both from us.

Like many people, I felt for a long time that I had to take care of myself because of the abuse in my childhood. It seemed that there wasn't anyone who truly cared for me. I felt as if I lived on guard, always watching out for the next painful event that would come my way. I couldn't trust my parents, and although I reached out to a couple of other relatives and asked for help, they didn't want to get involved. Incest in those days was unheard of. It was happening in a lot of families, but no one talked about it. It was so despicable that people didn't even want to think about it, let alone be involved in a situation where it was occurring.

I didn't feel loved, and when we don't feel loved we will feel insecure and lack confidence. When I was eighteen years old, I married the first young man who showed any interest in me.

After five years of his unfaithfulness and abandoning me several times, I divorced him, but my insecurity and lack of confidence grew even worse. I desperately needed to find love, but like most wounded people I continued to look for it in all the wrong places. I was dating a man who was a heavy drinker and was on my way to another disaster when I met Dave, to whom I have been married for more than fifty-three years.

Dave was the first person who showed me unconditional love, but I was so broken and wounded in my soul that I didn't even know what love was, nor did I know how to receive it. I lived in fear of the next disaster I was sure would befall me. The night Dave asked me to marry him, he told me he needed to talk to me about something before he took me home from our date, and I thought, *Here it comes. He is going to break up with me.* I never expected anything good to happen to me, but Dave's coming into my life was one of the best things that ever happened because he has not only loved me unconditionally, but he has also modeled the character of Christ. We endured several rough years, filled with my angry outbursts and negativity, but he stuck by me.

He was a strong Christian when I met him, and we went to church regularly, but several more years passed before I started letting God into the painful places in my life that needed healing. Eventually I did learn how much and how perfectly God loved me, and that gave me security and confidence.

> I waited patiently for the Lord; he turned to me and heard my cry. He lifted me out of the slimy pit, out of the mud and mire; he set my feet on a rock and gave me a firm place to stand.
>
> Psalm 40:1–2

Stop Listening to Lies

The devil puts all kinds of thoughts, which are lies, in our minds, and if we believe them, they will become our reality. He may have you convinced that you are just a shy person who lacks confidence and there is nothing you can do about it. Or, you may have accepted "insecure" as simply the way you are. Until we learn better, we usually just accept things that make us miserable as simply the way things are without even resisting them. Have you ever wondered how many lies you might believe that are adversely affecting your life? I never did until I started learning God's Word and discovered that His plan for me was much, much better than what I was experiencing.

> Have you ever wondered how many lies you might believe that are adversely affecting your life?

I had grown up in an atmosphere of total fear, and that was all I knew. I think it is safe to say that fear was my constant companion, and it manifested in all kinds of ways. Lacking security and confidence were only two of them, but there were many others. Fear of lack, fear of what people would think of me, fear that God was angry with me because of all my failures, and others. I had fears I didn't even realize I had because they had been with me all of my life. That may be true for you, too.

As you study God's Word, pay close attention to the life He wants you to have. If you don't have it, then begin confronting the devil's lies and defeating them one by one through God's truth. Jesus said often that He wants our joy to be full (John 15:11; 16:24; 17:13), so if you lack joy, you're not living your best life.

God doesn't want us to worry. Worry comes from insecurity

and the fear that you won't be taken care of, and it is rooted in the devil's lies. God promises to take care of us if we trust Him.

> Keep your lives free from the love of money and be content with what you have, because God has said, "Never will I leave you; never will I forsake you." So we say with confidence, "The Lord is my helper; I will not be afraid. What can mere mortals do to me?"
>
>   Hebrews 13:5–6

God is faithful, He cannot lie, and He is always the same. If He promises something, He never fails to do His part, but we do need to trust Him in order to receive and experience the good life He has for us. Developing a loving and trusting relationship with God through Jesus takes time, but as you faithfully study His Word and spend time with Him, you will grow spiritually in every way.

Before anything in our lives can change, we must know the truth, and we find it in God's Word. His Word is truth! Jesus said He is the Way, the Truth, and the Life (John 14:6). As our eyes are opened to more of the truth, we can experience more of what God has for us and not simply settle for what we've always known.

If you are insecure or lack confidence, don't just accept that as the way you are or the way it has to be. Submit to God; resist the devil and he will flee (James 4:7). When we have allowed something tormenting to remain in our lives because we didn't know we could be free from it, it's so exciting to realize the truth about God's desire and His plan to give us something so much better. But knowing the truth is only step one. Applying it to our lives must happen next.

Use Your Faith

If you need to overcome insecurity and a lack of confidence, the key to success is to put your faith in God and, as He leads you, step out into new things you have been afraid to do before. If you have lacked the confidence to pursue a promotion at work, go ahead and apply for the position for which you believe you are qualified. If you don't get the job, remain confident that God has just the right thing for you and keep stepping out. Eventually you will step into the perfect situation for you.

If you are lonely because you have been too insecure to try to make friends with people, start stepping out and being friendly. Don't sit by and wait for invitations; be the invitation! Reach out to others—chances are, they are lonely, too. The more you use your faith, the stronger it will become. Faith is confidence in God. It is said to be "the substance of things hoped for, the evidence of things not seen" (Heb. 11:1 NKJV). In other words, when you have faith that something will take place, you have it in your heart first (you believe), and then you will have it in reality in God's perfect timing.

> *The more you use your faith, the stronger it will become.*

Ask God for what you want and need. His Word says, "You do not have because you do not ask God" (James 4:2). God is able to do far more than we could ask or think (Eph. 3:20). In other words, you cannot ask God for too much. If what you ask for isn't right for you, He won't give it to you. But at the right time, He will give you something better.

This scripture is very encouraging to me, and I hope it will be to you, too:

Therefore I tell you, whatever you ask for in prayer, believe that you have received it, and it will be yours.

Mark 11:24

First we believe and then we receive. This verse does not tell us how much time will elapse between asking and receiving. We usually have to wait a while, and as we do, our faith is tested. But at the right time, God shows Himself strong and our prayer is answered if what we are asking for is God's will.

Faith is very powerful, and the force of it, when released, will help us overcome fear. I teach that we release our faith by praying, saying, and doing. In other words, faith is released when we pray, asking for God's help. It is also released when we declare God's Word out of our mouths. We must say what God says if we want to have what God wants to give us. Taking faith-filled action also releases faith.

Each time you see a prayer answered, it increases your confidence, and each time you step out to do something and experience success, that also increases your confidence. The more confidence you have, the more secure you will be. Watching God work in your life is not only exciting, it also makes you feel secure. We believe God loves us unconditionally because He repeatedly says in His Word that He does, but it also helps when we see the love of God manifested in our lives through things He does for us, even if they seem small.

The apostle Paul prayed for the Ephesians to know and experience God's love in a deep and intimate way (Eph. 3:17–19). I encourage you to expect and be on the lookout for God's love to show up in your life. Try not to miss one thing He does. God often works through people, so when someone you know does something

> *Expect and be on the lookout for God's love to show up in your life.*

kind for you, it is actually God loving you through them. Ponder often all the prayers God answers for you.

Just this morning Dave hurt his back and could barely move. But we prayed, and he took an anti-inflammatory medication and used ice on and off. It has been five hours, and he is amazingly better. His back is only a little tight now. That's answered prayer!

I had something in my eye that caused a great deal of pain. As I prayed about it, I had the thought that my neck might be causing the pain because my ear on that side had also been hurting. I put a heating pad on my neck and soon my eye did not hurt anymore. Another answered prayer!

God is so amazing, but sadly, for many years God did things like this for us, but we didn't give Him the credit He deserved. Now I know such experiences are God reaching into the practical aspects of my daily life and showing me His love. I urge you to watch for God's love, because doing so will really increase your faith, confidence, and security.

You Are Safe with God

The easiest way for me to define security is to say it is a feeling of safety. I think that is what I was missing in my childhood. I never felt safe. But God has redeemed me from that, and now I feel safe. I believe I have God's promise that He will always take care of me, and He will always take care of you, too.

> In peace I will lie down and sleep, for you alone, Lord, make me dwell in safety.
>
> Psalm 4:8

I love this scripture, because when I was a child I never lay down to sleep feeling safe. I never knew when my father would come into my room and put his hands in places they should not have been. Now when I go to sleep, I know I will be safe.

In our world today, we might be tempted to feel unsafe or insecure. It seems that violence is increasing worldwide. We hear of random shootings at shopping malls, theaters, and schools. You might ask, "Why didn't God keep those people safe?" I admit I don't know why, but I don't want the bad things in the world to keep me from seeing the good. If we only listen to the media and even to casual conversation all around us, it seems all we hear are the bad things, but there are good things, too. The devil just doesn't want us to notice them or talk about them.

> I don't want the bad things in the world to keep me from seeing the good.

We don't have a guarantee that we will never have trouble in our lives, but we are guaranteed that God will always be with us, and He will comfort and encourage us (Ps. 23:4; Isa. 41:10).

God tells us in His Word not to fret over evildoers because they shall soon be cut down like the grass. We are to trust in the Lord and keep doing good (Ps. 37:1–3). Let's try to focus more on what God says than on what the world says.

What a wonderful thing it is to feel secure and confident! This does not mean we will never have a problem, but that we will come through it into a place of safety. God says that when we go through difficulties, He will be with us:

> Do not fear, for I have redeemed you; I have summoned you by name; you are mine. When you pass through the waters, I will be with you; and when you pass through

the rivers, they will not sweep over you. When you walk through the fire, you will not be burned.

Isaiah 43:1–2

The "going through" is not enjoyable for us, but the promise of coming out of the problem gives us hope, confidence, and security. These are our gifts from God, and we should never leave a gift unopened. It is time to step up, step out, and show the devil just how big your God is!

PART 3

Mindsets for Walking in Freedom from Fear

Love is the master key that opens the gates of happiness, of hatred, of jealousy, and, most easily of all, the gate of fear.

Oliver Wendell Holmes Sr.

Fear Is a Liar

It was only seven thirty a.m., and I could already feel a familiar wave of anxiety and fear. Whenever my husband, Ed, traveled, fear would grip my heart at night. I would think, *Why now? He's been traveling for years! Why am I afraid all of a sudden?* I tried to work the same routine to ward off fear: Deny the fear, take melatonin, and pray. The only thing that seemed to give me a little bit of peace was to lock the bedroom door.

After a night of being on edge, I felt shame and frustration. *How can I talk to others about faith in a loving God and the power of prayer when I'm afraid of some unrealistic boogeyman?* I asked myself. I felt like a sham as a believer, someone who had no business talking to anyone about a life in Christ. I couldn't even muster the courage to tell anyone about my fear—including Ed.

With another trip coming up, I decided to call a counselor I had seen several years earlier. She had lovingly helped me look to God for healing of much past hurt and abuse. I told her of the shame and frustration of my nighttime terror.

She listened patiently and responded, "Joan, do you remember what you told me your brother used to say to you when you were kids before you went to bed at night?"

It was like a light bulb went on in my head. I said, "Yes! He said, 'You better lock your bedroom door tonight, because you never know what I might do.'"

My counselor reminded me that though I was helpless to do anything about the terror then, Ed is the safest person in my life. So, when he traveled, the old familiar pattern started again: helplessness, fear, shame, unwavering fear. For me, locking the door was the old answer to an old lie. Within months, I not only started sleeping with the door unlocked but wide open! I replaced the lie of fear with the truth of the victory that is mine in God who adores me. I have nothing to fear because I can rest in His love.

—Joan

CHAPTER 14

You Can Love Fearlessly

Freedom from the Fear of Letting Yourself Love

There is no fear in love [dread does not exist], but full-grown (complete, perfect) love turns fear out of doors and expels every trace of terror!

1 John 4:18 AMPC

Many people are afraid to love because they fear being hurt. Love requires being vulnerable, and that is very frightening to anyone who has loved and been badly hurt, betrayed, or abused by someone they loved and who said they loved them. My father told me all the time how much he loved me, but his kind of love allowed him to sexually abuse me. My mother said she loved me, but she abandoned me. And my first husband said he loved me, but he was unfaithful. By the time I met Dave, I didn't even know what love was, nor did I know how to give or receive it.

Only after learning to receive God's love and through trusting Him was I finally able to start trusting people who said they loved me. I won't say that those who love us will never hurt us, because in all probability they will. Sadly, as humans we hurt and disappoint one another, but through walking with God we find the grace to forgive and continue building healthy relationships.

I love Dave very much, but there are times when he disappoints me or hurts my feelings. When that happens, I have learned to go to God and receive the comfort and healing I need. I know Dave loves me and doesn't hurt me on purpose.

Many of our hurt feelings come from our unrealistic expectations. We may expect someone to do something for us, but they don't know we are expecting it, so they don't do it. How often, when you get hurt, do you think or say, "I *expected* more out of you than this," or "I sure didn't *expect* you to do that," or "I *expected* you to do that." God's Word teaches us that loving others means we believe the best of people (1 Cor. 13:4–7), and if we are willing to do that, we can avoid a lot of emotional pain.

> Many of our hurt feelings come from our unrealistic expectations.

When we learn to live without letting our fears determine our decisions and actions, we can love fearlessly. Even though we may feel cautious or even fearful, we can take a step of faith. I often say, "Step out and find out." Don't withdraw from others or isolate yourself, thinking that is the only way to be safe. All isolation does is cause us to live lonely, unfulfilled lives. God created us to need other people, and even though we are all different, we complete each other when we celebrate life together.

As we have already seen, the Bible teaches us that the perfect love of God casts out fear (1 John 4:18). Receiving God's love gives us courage to love others. Millions of people are desperate for someone to love them, and we can say, "God, use me." We can be the ones who allow God's love to flow through us to them. Just as His love heals us, His love through us can heal others.

Without Love There Is No Life

> We know that we have passed from death to life, because
> we love each other. Anyone who does not love remains in
> death.
>
> 1 John 3:14

The "each other" mentioned in this verse refers to those who belong to God through faith in Him. This scripture is powerful, not one to be passed over quickly. Think about what it is saying. If we don't love, we are held in death. That doesn't mean that we are not alive, but it does mean that we have no real life, no joy or peace. We are members of what I call the "walking dead." We exist, but life seems meaningless. Since we are created for love, we can never be truly happy without it. Dick Van Dyke, a famous actor who is more than ninety years old, said that no matter how old we are, "We all need something to do, someone to love, and something to hope for." I would also add that we need God, but I agree with what Van Dyke said.

First John includes several amazing scriptures about love. For example, "No man has at any time [yet] seen God. But if we love one another, God abides (lives and remains) in us and His love... is brought to completion...in us!" (1 John 4:12 AMPC). To *abide* means to live, dwell, and remain; since God is love, as we love others, God is present. His love is perfected in us. That means the cycle of love is completed. Love comes from God, is received by us, and flows through us back to God and to others. "We love because he first loved us" (1 John 4:19).

> Love comes from God, is received by us, and flows through us back to God and to others.

Whatever else our purpose is

for being on earth, our primary purpose is to let God's love flow through us. "And this is his command: to believe in the name of his Son, Jesus Christ, and to love one another as he commanded us" (1 John 3:23). We often wonder what God expects of us, and this one scripture sums up His expectations. You might ask, "What about obedience? Isn't that the most important thing?" The secret is that if we truly love God and others, we will obey. Perhaps we should focus more on what we should be doing (loving God and people) instead of what we should not be doing (sinning). What we focus on becomes what we produce in our lives. Paul told the Galatians that if they would walk in the Spirit, they would not fulfill the lusts of the flesh (Gal. 5:16). He didn't say, "Try not to fulfill the lusts of the flesh so then you can walk in the Spirit."

Focus on God and how much He loves you. Focus on loving Him and loving others, and many of your problems will disappear. All too often we focus on what others (including God) can and should be doing for us, but we should focus on what we can do for God and for others. It seems to me that we have a lot of things backward, and a little adjustment would be very helpful.

When you pray, try not to begin your prayer time by giving God a list of what you need Him to do for you. Instead, start by thanking Him for what He has already done for you, and then ask how you can serve Him and what you can do for Him and others. Think of someone you can bless and go do it. The less time we spend focused on ourselves, the happier we will be.

The Christian life is meant to be a flowing river, not a stagnant pond. Every good thing God gives us should flow through us to others. Walking in love with others is very important to God because that is the way the world will know Him (John 13:35). We are told to love the "brothers" (our fellow Christians), but

God also wants us to love all people—all kinds of people, even the ones who are not easy to love. Love isn't a feeling we wait to have; it is a decision we make about how we will treat people. You may not feel like helping someone in need if that person has hurt you, but loving is what God would do, and He expects us to represent Him in the earth.

Love's Requirement

Loving others requires us to learn how to live unselfishly, without constantly trying to take care of ourselves in ways that ensure that we will always get what we want. I don't know about you, but I am the kind of person who wants what I want, and if I am not careful, I could easily run over people to get it. I wish I were naturally a more selfless, sacrificing person, but that is not my natural temperament, so I have had to learn how to be unselfish on purpose by making choices to put others first. One of the most helpful scriptures I go to when I am battling thoughts that stir up the attitude *What about me?* is in Philippians:

> Do nothing out of selfish ambition or vain conceit. Rather, in humility value others above yourselves, not looking to your own interests but each of you to the interests of the others.
>
> Philippians 2:3–4

I want to clarify that this does not mean we are to view other people as better than ourselves, but we are to see them as being very important to God and treat them as such. We should never think

> "Do not think of yourself more highly than you ought." (Rom. 12:3)

we are better than others. Paul said it this way, "Do not think of yourself more highly than you ought" (Rom. 12:3).

This passage in Philippians also does not suggest that we should always give up our own desires in the interest of doing what someone else wants us to do. A person with an unbalanced attitude in this area can easily be controlled and manipulated. The goal is to be led by the Holy Spirit, asking God each day to help you not to be selfish, but to be available to help others.

Some of the ways we can help people are obvious. We should not even need to think about them for very long or pray about them, asking God if they are things He wants us to do. For example, when there is an elderly person in a grocery store line behind us with two items in their cart and ours is completely filled, we should know instinctively to let them go in front of us. I'm sure Jesus would. If we see a woman who is advanced in pregnancy pushing a loaded grocery cart while trying to hold her toddler by the hand and get to her car, we should offer to push the cart and load the groceries into her vehicle. If someone is walking in front of us on the sidewalk and they drop their shopping bag, causing several items to spill out and roll in different directions, human kindness dictates that we begin to collect the items in an effort to help the person. These types of actions are often referred to as "random acts of kindness." They are things we do simply because they are the right things to do. Nothing helps us keep our minds off of ourselves more than keeping them on others. Looking for opportunities to give, to serve, and help others everywhere we go and in all that we do brings death to the fleshly traits of selfishness and self-centeredness, and it brings life to our spirit.

Sometimes God sets up circumstances just to test us. He often does this when we are in a huge rush. That is when we have to make a decision: Is my tight timeline more important in this situation than showing the kindness of God?

One of our great fears in life is that we will not get what we want. This is why we try to control circumstances, people, and sometimes even God. We should focus more on giving than getting, and as we do, we will be happier people who put a smile on God's face. Little acts of kindness could change the world if everyone were committed to doing them.

> One of our great fears in life is that we will not get what we want.

It Is Difficult to Help Some People

Some people are difficult to help. Even though they need help, they are afraid to receive it because they don't want to feel indebted to anyone. It is a bit embarrassing when we try to help and are flatly refused. It may feel like a slap in the face, or at the very least, we feel rejected.

I recall once trying to pay for coffee for someone in line in front of me at Starbucks. She looked as though I had frightened her and refused to let me buy her a cup of coffee. I guess in today's society, with all its random acts of violence, she could have been afraid because she didn't know what my true motive was. But I feel sorry for people who don't know how to receive help or gifts. After that incident, I found myself feeling fear the next few times I started to do a random act of kindness, so I had to do it afraid! We cannot stop giving because some people don't know how to receive. Let's defeat random acts of violence with random acts of kindness.

Tear Down the Walls

When someone hurts me, the first thing I am tempted to do is to erect an invisible wall, one that stands between myself and the person who hurt me. I find myself thinking, *You won't get a chance to hurt me again. I will shut you out of my life, and that way you can't hurt me.* However, God wants us to give people another chance, just as He gives us, and sometimes another and another and another. The price Jesus paid for our freedom was pain, and if we want to enter into the amazing mystery of being loved and being loving, we will have to be willing to be hurt at times. God will be our wall of protection if we will stop building our own walls and instead put our trust in Him. I don't think it is possible to love and never be hurt, but Jesus, who is our healer, lives in us, and He binds up all of our wounds and heals our bruises (Ps. 147:3).

Fearless love will defeat our enemy, Satan, who is hard at work spreading strife and hatred to levels most of us have never witnessed before in our lifetime. We have to fight back, and the only thing that overcomes evil is good (Rom. 12:21). Walking in love is spiritual warfare and it makes us happy because Jesus Himself said, "It is more blessed to give than to receive" (Acts 20:35).

Most fears of rejection rest on the desire for approval from other people. Don't base your self-esteem on their opinions.

Harvey Mackay

The Fear I Didn't See Coming

When I was young, my whole life revolved around sports. As one sports season ended, another began. In middle school, I looked up to the high school football players at Friday night games and would think, *I'll be just like them one day!*

Being good at sports was also the only area in which my dad and I connected. He wasn't very affectionate, and the only time I felt like he was proud of me was when I succeeded in the classroom or on the field. Since I wasn't very academic, being good at sports was the only way to win his approval.

As my freshman year approached, I was eager and ready to try out for football and basketball. Days before the tryouts, my knee gave out, and I had to see a doctor. At the appointment, the doctor looked over his glasses and said the three words no athlete wants to hear: "You need surgery." And though that was a tough pill to swallow, I reminded myself that it was only freshman year. My life-long dream would not be denied; it would simply have to wait.

At the start of my junior year, my other knee gave out, and that led me right back to the same situation: major surgery, missing out on sports, and trying to stay positive. This is the exact moment when fear started to overtake me. I thought, *Will I ever be able to live my dream that I've worked so hard for? Will I still have friends if I can't play sports? What will my dad think? Will he still be proud of me? Will he still love me?*

Though I wish I could say that was the last time I had to deal with fear or another surgery, both would be wrong. I had to not only overcome the fear of missing out or the unknown (what I loved was taken away), but I also had to find my sense of security and purpose in Christ instead of in my abilities.

—Davis

CHAPTER 15

You Can Live in Acceptance

Freedom from the Fear of Rejection

Whoever listens to you listens to me; whoever rejects you rejects me; but whoever rejects me rejects him who sent me.

Luke 10:16

I would like to address specific fears in this book, but I know I can't get to all of them; therefore, I have chosen to write about the ones I think afflict the most people. There are all kinds of phobias that range from common ones to very unusual ones. One person may be afraid of heights, while another is afraid of butterflies, and another is afraid of bad weather. But no matter what kinds of fear people face, it all comes from one source, which is the devil. We need to say goodbye to all fear and learn to resist it at its onset. The longer we allow something to remain in our lives, the more deeply rooted it becomes and the harder it is to get rid of.

My Personal Experience

I had a longtime root of rejection in my life because I spent years feeling unloved. God created us for acceptance and love, not for abuse and rejection. When you experience rejection, be assured that Jesus knows just how you feel because He too was rejected by some of His family, His disciples, and the religious leaders of

> God created us for acceptance and love, not for abuse and rejection.

His day. Satan's plan was to use the pain of rejection to prevent Jesus from finishing what God sent Him to earth to do.

> He was despised and rejected by mankind, a man of suffering, and familiar with pain. Like one from whom people hide their faces he was despised, and we held him in low esteem.
>
> Isaiah 53:3

I doubt that any of us has ever or will ever experience the amount of rejection Jesus experienced, but other people's rejection didn't change Him. He knew He was God's Son, He knew what He had come to earth to do, and He kept His eyes on His Father's love for Him rather than on the rejection of people. We need to learn to do the same.

When I use the phrase *root of rejection*, I mean that a person has suffered so much rejection that the fear of it affects everything they do. People with a root of rejection often live very unhappy lives. They may believe they are being rejected and that people don't like or love them when that is not the case at all. Marilyn Monroe once said, "I feel like my whole life has been one big rejection." That is an interesting statement for a popular movie star to make. How could she have felt rejected when so many people sought after her, wanted to know her, and wanted her picture or autograph?

Her childhood was very difficult. Her mother was mentally ill, and her father was absent. She spent her youth in a series of foster homes and orphanages. It seems that as an adult, she never moved beyond the rejection and pain of those early lonely years. We know from most accounts that Marilyn Monroe lived a very unhappy life. She was in and out of relationships with a variety of men, many of whom were married. She died at age thirty-six of a barbiturate overdose.

It is interesting to note that some of Marilyn Monroe's most famous movies were comedies. I have heard stories of well-known comedians who were funny when performing, but in their daily lives they were unhappy and depressed. They played a role for people, which brought joy and laughter, but didn't enjoy their own lives at all.

One celebrity who was a comedian onstage but was reportedly anything but funny in real life was Lucille Ball. I have heard that she was one of the rudest and most unpleasant actresses to deal with in real life. She was said to have had a mean streak and a very complex personality and to have been quite insecure, which is a manifestation of a root of rejection.

I have known people who constantly joke around. Everything they hear evokes some comment from them that is meant to be funny, but they often go too far and it is annoying. I know this is not always the case, but many times people take on the comedian role in relationships because they are deeply insecure and feel they would be rejected if people knew who they truly are. I also know people who are truly humorous; it's simply part of their personality, not due to any problem they have.

I have personal experience with the root of rejection. I not only experienced rejection in my childhood by those who should have loved me, but it seemed to be a pattern in my life. I think I was rejected at times because, due to the pain in my childhood, my personality came across as rather unpleasant. I wasn't a person who was easy to be with or to like. When I met Dave, he accepted me unconditionally, but until that happened, I didn't know what that kind of acceptance felt like.

God Will Never Reject You

In John 6:37, Jesus said that those who come to Him will never be cast out or rejected. We can take that one Bible verse and let it deliver us from the fear of ever having God reject us for any reason. God loves us unconditionally, and that truth is often hard to grasp. Most of what we get in this world is based on our fulfilling certain conditions, but that is not the case in our relationship with God. God is love, and loving us is not something He does or doesn't do based on our behavior.

> Jesus said that those who come to Him will never be cast out or rejected.

One of the most important things for us to know is how much God loves us and how He sees us. If we have confidence in His love, we will never let the pain of rejection or the fear of other people control us or our decisions.

In his *Reflections for Ragamuffins*, Brennan Manning tells the story of a priest visiting family in Ireland. After watching the sunrise over Lake Killarney with his elderly uncle, the priest noticed a big smile on his uncle's face and commented, "Uncle Seamus, you look very happy."

His uncle answered, "I am."

When the priest asked why, the uncle simply stated, "The Father of Jesus is very fond of me."

We may be inclined to think this man's statement was filled with pride and ask, "Who does this guy think he is?" But the apostle John said many times that he was the disciple whom Jesus loved (John 19:26; 20:2; 21:7, 20). He was so confident in God's love that it became his identity. When asked who he was, he did not say he was a disciple, an apostle, or an evangelist. He simply said, "I am the disciple whom Jesus loves." The interesting thing is that all of us can say that, and we would all be right! We can all say, "God is very fond of me," "I am the apple of God's eye" (Ps. 17:8), or "I am God's favorite" and be correct. God doesn't just see us as a large mass of human beings; He sees and deals with us as individuals.

I believe that thinking more about how much God loves us and all the amazing things He says about us in His Word will boost our confidence to the point that we will never fear anyone's rejection or disapproval.

God says He created us, but the devil wants us to think we are an accident or a mistake. The truth is, with God's own hand He fashioned us in our mother's wombs, and we are made in His image (Ps. 139:13; Gen. 1:26–27). This thought provokes me to say, "Wow!" God values each of us, and we are precious in His sight. After God finished creation, including Adam and Eve, He saw that "it was very good" (Gen. 1:31). God sees us as good. All of our actions may not be good, but the part of us that He created is good.

The Bible does tell us not to think more highly of ourselves than we ought to (Rom. 12:3), but not thinking highly enough of ourselves can also be a problem. We have to find the right balance. We should know that in and of ourselves we are nothing without Christ, but through Him we are amazing creatures with God-given abilities. We are all infinitely different with different fingerprints and DNA. I heard last night that no two people have the same swirl or pattern in the irises of their eyes.

I will praise You, for I am fearfully and wonderfully made;
marvelous are Your works, and that my soul knows very
well.

Psalm 139:14 NKJV

David declared that he knew very well that he was fearfully
and wonderfully made. He knew he wasn't junk or trash or someone unimportant. He recognized what God had done in creating
him, and it was so amazing that when he said it was "fearful,"
he meant it was almost too amazing to even talk about. I would
definitely say after looking at some of the things the patriarchs
and the disciples and apostles said about themselves that most of
us have a long way to go in realizing just how amazing we are in
God's eyes.

At the end of the day, most people's self-image depends largely
on the messages they have received from other people. Am I
okay? Do they like me? Does anyone love me? Do I measure up
to what my family and friends expect? Like starving people, we
await others' nods of approval or a few words letting us know
they approve. But, in light of what God says about us, it is sad
that we hunger for people's approval considering that we already
have God's approval.

In the Book of Life—God's Word—the name of Peter, the man
who cursed and denied even knowing Jesus three times, is written right along with the name of John, who declared himself to
be the disciple whom Jesus loved (Matt. 26:69–75; John 20:2).
The name of Mary Magdalene, a woman who had seven demons
cast out of her, was written right along with the name of Mary,
the mother of Jesus, who is often referred to as the Blessed Vir-
gin (Luke 1:26–35, 48; 8:2). My name and your name are written

right along with all those who were crucified or burned at the stake or eaten by lions for refusing to deny their faith.

Positive Think Sessions

I want to encourage you to do something that may seem odd at first, but I know it will be very beneficial if you will do it. Do you know that you have the ability to think thoughts on purpose? You don't have to just wait to see whatever falls into your mind and then think it.

The apostle Paul instructs us to cast down imaginings, reasonings, theories, arguments, and lofty opinions that don't agree with God's Word (2 Cor. 10:5). This tells us that we can get rid of a thought we don't want and choose one that we do want.

I challenge you to have a five- or ten-minute think session every day during which you think about yourself the way God does. Think and declare these Scripture-based confessions:

> I challenge you to have a five- or ten-minute think session every day during which you think about yourself the way God does.

- I am the apple of God's eye (Ps. 17:8).
- I am fearfully and wonderfully made (Ps. 139:14).
- God rejoices over me with singing (Zeph. 3:17).
- I am precious in God's eyes (Isa. 43:4).
- I have been given the mind of Christ (1 Cor. 2:16).

You can begin with these suggestions, but I urge you to add to the list. Do some homework and find more scriptures that tell you how amazing you are. As you read and confess and meditate on these truths, they will change your image of yourself. Doing this will also help you see the people around you in a new and more positive light.

Most of us have thought too much about all the negative words people have spoken to us throughout our lives. I can remember my father telling me many times, "You will never amount to anything!" I remember making mistakes and being told I could not do anything right. As a teenager, I was fifteen to twenty pounds overweight, and I wasn't asked on a date or to school dances. Even if someone had asked, my father wouldn't have allowed me to go. All of these things caused me to feel inferior and insecure. When I got older, friends told me I had the wrong personality to be in ministry.

I was so accustomed to rejection that I came to expect it. I was sure something was wrong with me. After all, if my own father wanted to have sex with me, it must have been due to a flaw in me, because other girls' fathers were not like that. At least that's what I thought at the time. I was sure I was the only girl in the world having that experience. Eventually, I found out there are more than we can count, but many are either too ashamed or too fearful to talk about it. For years, I had what seemed to be a record playing in my head repeatedly, saying, "What is wrong with me?"

I can't even express how I felt when I learned that Jesus had taken my sin and given me His "right" standing with God. He had made me righteous (2 Cor. 5:21)! I no longer had to keep trying to figure out what was wrong with me, and you don't either. It doesn't mean something is wrong with you if you can't do everything right, or if you make mistakes on a regular basis, or if you are not like everyone else. You are precious, created by God, and He has a good plan for your life, so shake off every negative thing you have been told, and be the best you that you can be.

Do You Believe?

One day a six-year-old girl was sitting in a classroom. The teacher was going to explain evolution to the children. The teacher asked a little boy named Tommy if he could see the grass outside.

"Yes, teacher, I see the grass."

The teacher said, "Tommy, go outside and look up and see if you can see the sky."

He returned in a few minutes and said, "Yes, I saw the sky."

The teacher asked, "Did you see God?"

"No, teacher, I didn't see God."

The teacher said, "Well class, that is my point. We cannot see God because He isn't there."

A little girl spoke up and wanted to know if she could ask the boy some questions. The teacher agreed, and the little girl asked: "Tommy, do you see the tree outside?"

"Yes, I see the tree."

She asked, "Do you see the grass?"

He said, "Yes, I see the grass."

"Do you see the sky? Do you see the teacher?"

Tommy said, "Yes," and his tone of voice indicated that he was tired of answering questions.

The little girl finally asked, "Do you see the teacher's brain?"

Tommy said, "No, I don't see her brain."

The little girl said, "Then according to what we were taught today, that means she must not have one."

Are you able to believe what you don't see simply because God says it is true? According to 2 Corinthians 5:7, we "walk by faith, not by sight" (NKJV). Faith believes what it cannot see yet, but believes it will be seen in due time. You or I may not be manifesting all the wonderful things God's Word says about us yet, but if we continue in His Word, we will. We will be transformed into the image of Christ (2 Cor. 3:18; Rom. 8:29). In God's Kingdom we must believe before we will see, but in the world we must see to believe. As God's children we can see things with the eyes of our hearts, and they are more real to us than things we see with our natural vision.

I believe with all of my being that Jesus died for my sins and rose from the dead. I didn't see it happen, but I know it is true beyond a shadow of a doubt. For that reason I have given my life to teaching this truth to others. I haven't seen God, but I regularly see the results of believing in Him and serving Him. One thing is for sure: Before Jesus my life was a total wreck, but now it is amazing!

After reading this chapter, I think we can all say there is no reason to fear the rejection of people, because God loves us and He is on our side. It is time to see ourselves the way God sees us and let His opinion of us be more important than what anyone else thinks.

A man who is intimate with God will never be intimidated by men.

Leonard Ravenhill

Choosing Not to Worry about Other People's Opinions of Me

Cake tastings, a guest list, a budget, dress fittings—all the details of planning a wedding are enough to drive anyone a little crazy! Throughout my engagement, though, I neglected to focus on the most important detail—my upcoming marriage. My fiancé and I were young and in love, and I assumed that since he went to church, he would make a great husband. You see, I'd been abused by boyfriends in the past and mistreated by just about every guy in my life, so when I became a Christian and started dating a guy from church, I thought he was the best I'd ever have.

My family and mentors from church warned me, though, that our relationship was toxic. He had been raised to look out for number one above all else, and while this didn't necessarily make him a terrible person, that mentality does not work well in a marriage.

I knew in my gut that I wasn't supposed to marry him, but I was completely terrified. Scared of being alone. Scared of losing someone I loved. Scared of the money I would waste and the embarrassment I would face. How would I explain to everyone on my "friends list" when my status went from "in a relationship" to "single"? The thought of all of it made me sick!

But then I remembered my worth in Christ. In Jeremiah 29:11, He promises hope and a good future. He wanted to prosper me, and by marrying someone who was just good enough, I wasn't allowing His blessing to take full effect.

So, I did it—*afraid.*

I wrote a long note, handed back my ring, and took a giant leap of faith into a whole new realm of trusting God. I was completely broken, yet wholly dependent on God. And wow, did He *show up*! I was blessed with incredible friends who swooped in to remind me that I'm not alone. I traded my time-consuming wedding planning for serving in the church and community, and I felt purpose like never before. And the most amazing thing happened—my fiancé did the same thing! He turned his life around and devoted himself to serving others instead of serving himself.

After a year of being apart from my fiancé, we started dating again, and less than a year later, I finally got to marry the man of my dreams. And this time, he fulfilled God's dreams for me, too. We now both serve as youth pastors at an inner-city church and get to help others overcome their fears and live that Jeremiah 29:11 life. All because I chose to do it afraid.

—Julie

CHAPTER 16

You Can Be Yourself

Freedom from the Fear of What Other People Will Think, Say, or Do

> *Fear of man will prove to be a snare, but whoever trusts in the Lord is kept safe.*
>
> Proverbs 29:25

Initially I intended to put the fear of rejection and the fear of what other people will think, say, or do in the same chapter because they are similar. But I think the fear of other people's opinions, words, and actions is such a huge problem that it deserves a chapter of its own. I suspect that more people deal with this fear than any other one. Wanting other people to like us is natural, but that desire becomes a problem when we want it so much that we allow people to control us in order to get it. Anyone can experience this fear, but those who have been emotionally wounded or abused in the past are likely to struggle with it more than others.

If we are plagued by the fear of what others will think, say, or do, we may merely let people control us by doing everything they want us to do because we are afraid they won't like us if we don't. I once had an employer who was very controlling, and I was careful not to confront him or to act as though I thought he was wrong about anything because I knew he would get angry.

My father was an angry man, and he controlled my mother and me through his anger. We lived under constant stress trying to keep him happy so that we wouldn't have to deal with his temper and outbursts of anger. Because of my experience with him, I developed a fear of making people angry, so it was easy for people to control me.

I also had a friend who was quick to anger, and I always did what she wanted to do, even if I didn't want to do it. Once again, allowing myself to be controlled was rooted in my fear of making people angry. I wasn't nearly as afraid of what they would say to me or about me, what they would do to me, or what they would think of me as I was of the anger they displayed. I still become uncomfortable when I am around someone who is easily angered, but I don't let it control me.

We may let people control us because they have something we want, and we know we won't get it if we confront them. Often, we won't confront people or be honest with them because we see them as having control over our future in some way. For example, a person may let an employer mistreat him or overwork him because he is afraid of losing his job. Or, a teenager may do things she knows are wrong just to be accepted by her peers. But, if we put our trust in God, He will control our future, and nobody will be able to prevent us from fulfilling our God-ordained destiny.

I encourage you to ask yourself if you are letting anyone control you due to the fear of what they may think, say, or do. If so, make the decision to break free from it. Letting it go on without confronting it is a trap that will make you miserable. Remember the verse at the beginning of this chapter: "Fear of man will prove to be a snare, but whoever trusts in the Lord is kept safe" (Prov. 29:25).

Don't Miss God's Best

God has a plan for each of us, and it is a very good plan. His is actually the best plan, but if we are people-pleasers instead of God-pleasers, we will miss the best and end up settling for whatever people try to give us.

God has a destiny for each of us, something He has assigned us to do in His Kingdom, but in order to fulfill that destiny, our desire to be popular and well liked must be submitted to our desire to fulfill His plan for our lives. We all want to be liked, loved, admired, accepted, and applauded, but we must beware of wanting these things so much that they cause us to disobey God.

The apostle Paul was one of the greatest apostles. He wrote approximately two-thirds of the New Testament and said that had he tried to be popular with people, he would not have become an apostle (Gal. 1:10). He would have missed out on all the joy of serving God the way he did.

I would venture to say that possibly millions of people have missed their destiny due to the fear of other people's thoughts, words, or actions. I have found in my life that every time God was about to promote me to a new level of ministry, the devil came against me with the disapproval of people I didn't want to lose in my life at that time. I suffered tremendously in this area until I finally realized that Satan was the one who instigated those attacks in an effort to keep me out of God's will.

> *It's possible that millions of people have missed their destiny due to the fear of other people's thoughts, words, or actions.*

When I first started teaching a Bible study in my home, family and friends who didn't believe women should teach the Bible ostracized me. God had touched my life in a profound way, and as I entered into a more intimate relationship with Him, I began to want His will more than anything else. I didn't expect those closest to me to be anything other than happy for me, but that turned out not to be the case.

It looked as though I was going to lose some friends if I was going to follow God. I have experienced that numerous times throughout my life, and I am sure you have, too. Satan uses the fear of rejection and disapproval, or the fear of what others will think or how they will respond to us, more than anything else to control us.

Finding Freedom

If we think about the heroes of our faith mentioned throughout the Bible, we notice that many of them had to confront the fear of others in order to become who God wanted them to be.

Moses, for example, was afraid the people wouldn't believe him if he told them God had sent him to lead them out of Egypt. He felt he wasn't a good speaker (Exod. 4:10; 6:30), and even after God promised to help him speak and teach him what to say (Exod. 4:12), he still tried telling God He had the wrong man and begged Him to send someone else (Exod. 4:13).

God eventually became angry with Moses and said to him: "What about your brother, Aaron the Levite? I know he can speak well. . . . You shall speak to him and put words in his mouth; I will help both of you speak and will teach you what to do. He will speak to the people for you" (Exod. 4:14–16). We can see from this example how extraordinarily patient God is with us.

There are instances when Moses did speak to the people for God, so at some point he must have gotten over his fear of speaking in front of people. Moses learned quickly that if he obeyed God, there would always be someone who didn't like his decision to do so. While Moses tried to lead the Israelites to the Promised Land, they grumbled their way through the wilderness. No matter what God or Moses did, the people seemed to find something to be unhappy about. I once read that 10 percent of all people won't like us no matter what we do. Reading that helped me, because it confirmed to me again that if I were going to follow God, there would always be someone who wouldn't like me or approve of my choices.

Joseph had a dream from God about his destiny, and when he shared it with his brothers they became jealous and sold him into slavery (Gen. 37). As I mentioned in an earlier chapter, God anointed David to be king, but Saul (who was king at the time) was jealous of David and hated him. He also spent many years trying to kill David. Moses, Joseph, and David all went on to fulfill their destinies even though they had to confront the fear of other people.

These men were great heroes of faith, yet they had to face their fears and overcome them, and so will we. The apostle Peter certainly wrestled with the fear of others' opinions because he denied knowing Jesus three times (Luke 22:54–62). This was during the time when the members of the Sanhedrin were questioning Jesus and when Pontius Pilate eventually sentenced Him to death. This was surely a situation when Jesus would have needed the support of His disciples, but Peter failed Him. Nevertheless, Jesus forgave Peter, and he went on to become a fearless and bold apostle.

We can see from these stories that the fear of what others will think, say, or do can attack anyone, no matter how close they are to God. We can also see that we can leave fear behind and become courageous and bold.

Be Yourself

You will either be yourself or you will try to be who and what other people think you should be. Only you can decide which it will be. You can have the joy of being true to yourself and following God as He leads you, or you can cower to the demands of people. Paul instructed us to work at whatever we do heartily as for the Lord and not for man, knowing that our reward will come from Him (Col. 3:23–24).

> *You will either be yourself or you will try to be who and what other people think you should be. Only you can decide which it will be.*

We may gradually, without even noticing it, slip into the trap of being people-pleasers. Wanting to please people is human nature and, in fact, God tells us that "no one should seek their own good, but the good of others" (1 Cor. 10:24). However, if meeting with their approval means we will displease God, we should always choose to please Him.

If you are doing things for people and you don't have peace about doing them, or you truly do not want to do them, ask yourself why you are doing them. God may ask you to do something you don't want to do for someone, and if that is your reason, then you are doing it to obey and please Him. But if you are doing it to keep that person from becoming angry or rejecting you, you are doing it for the wrong reason, and that displeases God.

I once attended a church that had little cliques in the congregation. Those who were considered "in" with the right people were invited to the right parties, recommended to be board members of the church, admired, and well informed about what was going on in the church. They also knew a lot about what was going on with most of the people who attended the church. I decided I wanted to be in that group, and although I wasn't aware of it at the time, I only wanted to be part of it because I was insecure and searching for value. Like most cliques, this one had a leader—a woman who controlled it—and in order to be invited into the group, I needed her to accept me.

I went to work paying compliments to the leader, most of which were not sincere, and I offered to help her anytime I could. Before long I was accepted, and it felt so good, but I know now that the situation wasn't pleasing to God. Actually, when God called me to teach His Word, she was one of the first people who judged me, rejected me, and talked bad about me. I gained her favor by doing everything she wanted, and the first time I did something she did not approve of, she turned against me.

In order to please her, I wasn't true to myself. Everyone we deal with expects something different out of us, so if we try to please all the people all the time, we will become confused, worn-out, frustrated, and unhappy. It is important for us to put everything we are about to do and each step we are about to take before God in prayer. Proverbs 3:6 says that if we acknowledge Him in all our ways, He will direct our path.

Motives are about *why* we do what we do, not just *what* we do, and they are very important to God. We are not to do good deeds in order to be seen, applauded, or well thought of. We should do what we do out of motives of obedience to God and because we love Him and we love others. Although God has told us that sincere giving will produce a harvest in our lives (Luke 6:38), enjoying a harvest is not the reason to give. We should give to bless people and to be obedient to God. Having pure motives always produces blessings from God, while impure motives do not.

I find sometimes that if I give something to someone and they don't thank me, I feel annoyed. Then I have to remember that it may just be God testing me to see if I did it to be thanked and well thought of or to simply be a blessing to someone else.

Trade Intimidation for Intimacy with God

> A man of too many friends comes to ruin, but there is a friend who sticks closer than a brother.
>
> Proverbs 18:24 NASB

This verse clearly says that if we try to be friends with everyone, we will come to ruin, but if we choose Jesus as our best friend, He will never disappoint us, leave us, or forsake us—even when we do something He doesn't like. He will correct us, but He won't reject us.

Preceding this chapter is a quote from Leonard Ravenhill, and I want to call your attention to it again: "A man who is intimate with God will never be intimidated by men." Why? Because intimacy with God brings clarity into our lives and enables us to see things as they really are. Intimacy with Him enables us to know our own hearts and discern whether or not our actions stem from pure motives. Intimacy with God shields us from being intimidated, manipulated, and controlled by people.

> "A man who is intimate with God will never be intimidated by men." (Leonard Ravenhill)

We know that David was the beloved of God (Ps. 60:5; 108:6). There was one thing he sought, which was to live in God's presence and behold His beauty all the days of his life (Ps. 27:4). This scripture had a major impact on my life, because I realized I was seeking many things, none of which was to live in God's presence. Naturally, I would have loved to do that, but I wasn't asking for it or seeking it, so it must not have been very important to me.

I was serving God in ministry and must admit that, at the time, I was quite proud of myself for doing so. One day God reminded me that although I was proud of myself for serving Him, I wasn't spending any time with Him, and that was what was important to Him. What we do for God means nothing if He is not first in our lives.

Jesus taught us to seek first the kingdom of God and then all the other things we need will be added to us (Matt. 6:33). Is God first in your life? Is He more important to you than getting the things you are asking Him to give you? If you had to give up everything in order to have God in your life, would you do that? Would I? I guess we don't know unless we are faced with that choice, but I hope and pray that I am close enough to Jesus that I would make the right choice, knowing that without Him I would be lost and miserable.

The longer we serve God, the more we learn and grow spiritually. If some of what you are reading seems daunting to you or represents a standard you think you could never measure up to, then the devil is lying to you. Every day you stick with Jesus, you learn a little something and become more and more addicted to His presence in your life. I cannot even imagine now how I managed all those years just going to church but never thinking about God in between services except to say a little prayer over meals and before going to bed at night. No wonder my life was falling apart, even though I was a churchgoing Christian. I once heard, "We should come apart and spend time with God before we literally come apart."

Spending time with God simply means talking with Him, thanking Him for His goodness in your life, praying about things that concern you, asking questions as you study His Word, sharing your concerns, and anything else you want to do. You may feel it is difficult to do that since you are speaking to someone you cannot see, but God can see you and loves to be invited into everything you do. You may not see God with your eyes, but you can see Him working in your life and in the lives of people around you. Every time that happens, it helps you to open your heart to Him even more.

Simply going to church week after week or even several times a week can become mundane (something done merely out of habit), but adding to faithful church attendance intimacy with God in your daily life makes a relationship with Him exciting and often mysterious. If we agree to follow God daily, we have to be ready to be surprised, because He may ask us to do something we never would have thought about doing.

Living in the Spirit and by the Spirit is a fresh, exciting way to live! If you are tired of trying to run your own life, choose your own friends, and please the people around you in unhealthy ways, let this be a turning point for you. One word from God can change your life, and if God is speaking to you through the words of this book, I urge you to let go of the fear of what other people will think, do, or say and take hold of friendship and true intimacy with God.

Men are swayed more by fear than by reverence.

Aristotle

Awesome!

Had anyone ever told me I would reach a point where I was afraid of God, I would have laughed. After all, I was raised to love Him and to believe He was an approachable Father who wanted the best for me.

Then, a time came when that belief was fiercely challenged. As a result of a situation people said was "God's will," I suffered a painful loss. The situation caused me to wonder if God was punishing me for some bad attitude or sinful behavior and to be afraid of what He might do next that would hurt me. For a season, I became afraid of Him in the way people might fear someone filled with rage or someone who poses a threat to their safety or well-being. He didn't feel safe anymore.

Over time, because of His relentless love, I began to see that the situation *really was* God's will. He turned the loss into great restoration and did a deep work of healing and strength in my heart. That's when my fear of Him, as we understand the word *fear* today, with all its negative connotations, became the kind of fear the biblical writers understood. When they wrote about "the fear of the Lord," they meant *fear* in the sense of overwhelming honor and reverence.

One contemporary term that may capture the heart of the phrase "the fear of the Lord" is awe. God is awesome—awesome in wisdom, awesome in love, awesome in forgiveness, and awesome in the way He heals us, sets us free, and works all things together for our good (Rom. 8:28). When we are afraid of Him in the way we think of fear today, we keep ourselves from experiencing these blessings. When we relate to Him from a position of fear, we find ourselves frustrated and confused. But when we begin to see Him for who He really is, we can't help but feel that biblical fear of the Lord and say, "God, You're awesome!"

—Beth

CHAPTER 17

You Can Trade Fear for Fear

Freedom from the Wrong Kinds of Fear

The fear of the Lord is the beginning of wisdom, and knowledge of the Holy One is understanding.

Proverbs 9:10

According to Proverbs 9:10, we don't really know anything until we know the most important thing there is: the reverential fear of God. All other kinds of fear are wrong types of fear and are to be resisted and overcome. But there is one fear that is right, and it is more valuable than we might imagine. I am talking about the reverential fear of God. It will set us free from wrong and tormenting fears. We can literally trade one kind of fear for another.

This is confusing to some people, because they have been taught a great deal about how much God loves them and how gracious and kind He is, so they cannot imagine needing to fear Him. They get the part about being set free from wrong fears, but struggle when someone mentions the fear of God.

The reverential fear of God is completely different from other fears, and when we talk about it, the word *fear* is used in an entirely different context than it is when we talk about fear in terms of being frightened. Reverential fear is a respectful and awe-inspiring fear, one that says, "I know God is all-powerful and that He means what He says. He is good. He loves me, and He will always take care of me." The emphasis is on reverence and awe, not our common modern-day understanding of fear. If He says, "Do this and you will be blessed," we can know without doubt that if we follow Him, blessings will follow us. Likewise, if God says, "If you do this other thing, things will not go well," we should know that He also means exactly what He says and will not make an exception for anyone.

Joy Dawson writes in her book *Forever Ruined for the Ordinary*, "The fear of the Lord means being more impressed with God's reactions to our actions than with other people's reactions." I really like that statement, because if we care more about what God thinks of our actions than what people think, we won't fear them because we do fear Him.

Anyone can be forgiven for any sin. There is no limit to how many times a person may be forgiven. However, if we continue doing what we know is wrong, merely thinking we can do wrong and still get a right result, then we are disrespecting the commands of God. That never turns out well.

Reverential fear of God is greatly missing in the world today, but it is also missing in the hearts of many Christians. I personally believe it should be taught in every church at least once or twice a year because people lose sight of any subject that is not mentioned, even if it is important to the Christian life.

I know a lovely woman who is almost fifty years old. She has been in church all of her life and is in ministry herself, but when I mention the reverential fear of God, it confuses her. She doesn't think we should be afraid of God for any reason. I totally agree with her if we are talking about the wrong type of fear. We don't have to be afraid of God's anger, rejection, or punishment, but we do need to know He is sincere in everything He says and that we cannot just pick out the Bible verses we like and ignore the rest.

I can quickly locate at least thirty-two Bible verses related to the fear of God in the Old and New Testaments. If the scriptures are there, we cannot ignore the truth they present. We need to understand them and see if we are applying them to our lives.

John Newton (1725–1807), who penned the popular hymn "Amazing Grace," must have certainly understood the reverential fear of God, for he wrote these words in the song:

> 'Twas grace that taught my heart to fear,
> And grace my fears relieved;
> How precious did that grace appear
> The hour I first believed.

He had traded fear for fear! His revelation of the grace of God set him free from wrong fears but gave him reverential fear. John Newton had been the master of a slave ship. He once got caught in a terrible and terrifying storm and had a near-death experience at sea. That situation provoked him to cry out to God and convert to Christianity. He quickly saw the error of his ways and was amazed that God's grace totally forgave him. Ultimately, he fought against slavery and became an Anglican minister. Prior to knowing God, he had no fear of enslaving other people for his own profit. But as soon as he came to know God, he knew it was wrong. He would have actually been afraid to continue doing it because he didn't want to displease the God of all grace.

His revelation of the grace of God set John Newton free from wrong fears but gave him reverential fear.

How would you or I behave in the presence of Queen Elizabeth II of England? She isn't even my queen, but I would be very careful not to behave foolishly or inappropriately around her. I would do that because of reverence, knowing I was in the presence of someone great. Once we realize that we are always in God's presence and He sees and knows everything we do, we will also behave better, not because we are afraid He will punish us if we don't, but because we respect and revere Him.

Some Inappropriate Behavior

Today we live in what is considered to be a very casual society. Dress is casual; sadly, many times attitudes toward authority figures are casual; and people can be casual about arriving for appointments. People who have casual attitudes toward these things may also take those attitudes to church with them. Let me ask a few questions, and you can see for yourself what you think.

Should we be texting a friend in church while the pastor is speaking? Would we want someone to do that to us if we had studied and prepared a message we hoped would help people? If we believe God is speaking to and through the pastor, are we not being rude to not listen intently?

Should we regularly walk into services late and disturb people who are either trying to worship God or listen to the speaker? Anyone can be late occasionally, but if it is a regular habit, you might want to ask yourself if an attitude in your heart needs to be changed. Perhaps it has something to do with not having enough reverence for God.

Or how about walking out of the service while the pastor is giving an invitation for people to repent of their sins and receive Christ? Anyone who absolutely has to leave early should sit in the back row so they won't disturb what is happening when they get up. I know from personal experience in our conferences that sometimes hundreds of people get up and start filing out of the building while I am talking to people about eternity and inviting them to accept Christ as Savior. First and foremost, disrupting such a moment is rude to God, because salvation is the most important decision in a person's life. It is also rude to people who may be in the process of responding to the call to salvation and to those who are trying to pay attention or praying, and it is rude to the person leading the service.

If we are sitting in the middle of a row and get a little thirsty and decide to disturb twenty people just to get a drink of water, is that showing reverence to God? Anyone with a true emergency is free to leave at any time, but disturbing the service for a minor discomfort is, in my estimation, rude. The Bible says that love is not rude (1 Cor. 13:4–5). Think what a difference it would make in the world today if people just stopped being rude. Rudeness is the fruit of selfishness; it is all about what we want without having any concern for what others want or need.

Being from a different generation than many people today, I realize I might be a little old-fashioned, but I truly believe that in our effort to be modern, we may have let go of some things we should work at getting back.

I believe Scripture backs up the point that if we don't fear God, we won't respect people, either.

> In a certain town there was a judge who neither feared God nor cared what people thought.
>
> Luke 18:2

I remember days when basic respect and good manners dictated that a man would not curse in the presence of a woman.

No matter how much of a scoundrel he might be, he behaved as a gentleman while in the presence of women, especially ones he did not know. I am glad I lived in the times when a man's word was his bond and doing an excellent job was part of his honor and something that was very important to him. Even most men who did not claim to be Christians still held these principles. We had reverence for those in positions of authority, such as police officers, judges, teachers, employers, pastors, and others. Because God loves people so much and displayed that love in sending His Son to die for their sins and take the punishment they deserved, we should have reverential fear of mistreating anyone because we realize everyone is important to God.

> We should have reverential fear of mistreating anyone because we realize everyone is important to God.

How many people today strive to be excellent? Are most people satisfied with merely being mediocre? Recently at a conference, one of my teachings was on choosing to be excellent. After the teaching, a well-known Bible teacher who is probably in his mid-thirties and has been raised in church came to me and said, "I have never heard anything like that in all my life." He continued, "This will be life-changing for me." How can a person be in church all of his life and never hear about the importance of being excellent? We should always go the extra mile to do things the best way possible, because our God is excellent in all of His ways (Matt. 5:41).

Reverential Fear and Power

In its early days, the church throughout all of Judea and Galilee and Samaria had peace and was being built up. As the believers walked in the fear of the Lord and in the comfort of the Holy Spirit, the church grew and multiplied (Acts 9:31). I see a very important point in this scripture: *They walked in the fear of the Lord and they multiplied.* The fear of the Lord and church growth seemed to go hand in hand. Perhaps we need more fear of the Lord and fewer meetings on how to cause the church to grow.

We know that in the past some people with very public ministries have been convicted for misusing ministry finances. They have admitted to adultery, addictions to pornography, and using their power to control and mistreat other people, all while remaining in the pulpit and preaching to others regularly, telling them how to live their lives. These things could not have happened if those leaders had walked in a proper fear of the Lord. Either they would not have committed the sins to begin with, or if they had, they would have confessed and stepped down from their positions while seeking restoration.

Noah built the ark because he had reverence in his heart toward God (Gen. 6). Abraham was prepared to offer his son as a sacrifice when God told him to do so. This is what the Lord spoke to him: "'Do not lay a hand on the boy,' he said. 'Do not do anything to him. Now I know that you fear God, because you have not withheld from me your son, your only son'" (Gen. 22:12). Surely we would see more obedience in the lives of Christians if that same kind of fear of the Lord were present today. These were men with power, who did amazing things, and I think that is clearly linked to their reverential fear of God.

The apostle Peter offered a simple formula for Christians to live by: "Show proper respect to everyone, love the family of believers, fear God, honor the emperor" (1 Pet. 2:17).

The times we live in are what I would call "desperate times." More than ever, people need God but are turning away from the church as a source of finding Him. What answer can we give to this perplexing situation? Shouldn't people who want and need God be able to look to the church (Christians everywhere) for the help they need? Sometimes they do but end up disappointed because the lifestyles they witness don't match the message they hear.

There are many wonderful, amazing churches that represent God very well, and we honor and compliment them. They are the remnant keeping the flame of hope alive. But when it comes to Christlike behavior, it should never be "some people" or "some churches," but "all people" and "all churches."

If you feel the need for more power in your life or ministry, make sure you have a proper reverential fear and awe of God.

Two Kinds of Fear

John Newton sang that grace set him free from fear and taught him fear at the same time. I can understand people's confusion when the fear of God is mentioned, because many of them have suffered greatly with the wrong kind of fear of God.

Martin Luther distinguished the two types of fear by calling them the "servile" fear of God and the "filial" fear of God. Servile fear is what a prisoner would have toward a jailer who had the ability to torture him. It is also the kind of fear a person would have for a master who had the power to abuse him and often did. Filial fear is what a child would feel for loving parents, a child who loves his parents tremendously and wants with all of his heart to please them. This reverential fear is strong enough to move people to not merely do as they please if they know it is not what would please his parents.

The reverential fear of God will set us free from being in bondage to wrong fears. When the apostle John describes coming face-to-face with God, he said that

> The reverential fear of God will set us free from being in bondage to wrong fears.

he fell down as if he were a dead man (Rev. 1:17–18). He obviously reverenced God greatly.

David spoke of bowing toward God's holy temple and giving thanks (Ps. 138:2). We want to know the great *love* of God, but we also need to know the great *power* of God.

> "Vengeance is mine; I will repay." And again, "The Lord will judge his people." It is a fearful thing to fall into the hands of the living God.
>
> Hebrews 10:30–31 ESV

Why is it a "fearful thing" to fall into God's hands? God sees everything for exactly what it is. If there is any pretense, He sees right through it. God sees everything we do and knows everything about us. But He also loves us so much that if anything is not right, He will lovingly help us face and deal with it. We can often fool people with pretense, but not God. He works with us to obtain purity in all things.

God loves us too much to ever leave us alone in our sin. He will help us even if He has to lead us into some uncomfortable places to do so. I personally love the conviction of the Holy Spirit, and I take it as a sign of God's love, not as something I need to feel guilty about. When we do something sinful, have a wrong attitude, or mistreat someone, God will make us aware of our bad behavior, and that is really good because we cannot correct the faults that we do not see in ourselves. Let us pray that God will open our eyes and unstop our ears so we might see and hear Him clearly and have a deep reverential fear and awe of Him.

Wealth consists not in having great possessions, but in having few wants.

Epictetus

Pushing Past the What-Ifs

On my fortieth birthday, my wife and I were sitting on our patio when I said, "We need to decide once and for all about having children." We had been married for several years and had talked about starting a family from time to time, but never seriously.

My bright idea was that my wife could work from home and raise our children. Her idea was that I could leave my job and stay home. It made sense financially, but how could I do that? How would it look for a man to leave his job to stay at home with children and allow his wife to support the family? My wife asked me to please stop wondering about the opinions of millions of unknown people in the world and decide for myself if I thought it was something I could do. I knew I could, if I could get past my fear of people's opinions.

Fast-forward several months. We were expecting our daughter. I had given notice at work and planned to leave my job at the end of the year. I gave three months' notice, and in those three months, there were moments when I became paralyzed with fear.

I would think: *What if Celeste loses her job and we have no income? What if I can't do it? I don't know anything about raising a child! What if something happens to the child and I can't find another job? What if… What if… WHAT IF?????*

My last day at work was tough, and the fear I felt was incredible. However, I knew I had to do it afraid. After all, that was the only way to accomplish what God had called me to do.

I stayed home with our two children for nine years. It was the toughest, most challenging job I've ever had, but they were definitely nine of the best years of my life!

—Chuck

CHAPTER 18

You Can Stop Worrying about Money

Freedom from Financial Fears

And my God will meet all your needs according to the riches of his glory in Christ Jesus.

Philippians 4:19

Paul wrote these words to those who had entered into a faithful partnership with him in giving and receiving. They received from Paul's teaching ministry, from his love, and from his kindness, and he received from them finances to help him continue doing what he was doing for them and others.

The Bible includes many scriptures that teach us the benefits and duty of giving to others. If we do so regularly and with proper motives, God will always meet all of our needs. Paul said, "If we have sown spiritual seed among you, is it too much if we reap a material harvest from you?" (1 Cor. 9:11).

I could quote many Bible verses that teach us the blessings we can expect as generous givers, but I have chosen to focus here on one passage that I believe says it all:

Remember this: Whoever sows sparingly will also reap sparingly, and whoever sows generously will also reap generously. Each of you should give what you have decided in your heart to give, not reluctantly or under compulsion, for God loves a cheerful giver. And God is able to bless you abundantly, so that in all things at all times, having all that you need, you will abound in every good work. As it is written:

"They have freely scattered their gifts to the poor; their righteousness endures forever."

Now he who supplies seed to the sower and bread for food will also supply and increase your store of seed and will enlarge the harvest of your righteousness. You will be enriched in every way so that you can be generous on every occasion, and through us your generosity will result in thanksgiving to God.

2 Corinthians 9:6–11

This passage is easy to understand and, if obeyed, will produce the result it promises. We won't need to live with financial fears because we will see that God's Word is true. If you have fears concerning money, you might have to begin giving—and doing it afraid—and you will learn that God is faithful to His Word. You will also be able to enjoy watching Him take care of you instead of feeling the pressure of always having to take care of yourself.

In addition to giving to others, we must also use wisdom with the finances we have. Perhaps you are in financial difficulties because you have not given to help others or used wisdom in the past, but that can be easily corrected. Each time you do the right thing, you will overturn some of the result of the wrong things done in the past. God immediately and completely forgives all our

> Each time you do the right thing, you will overturn some of the result of the wrong things done in the past.

mistakes and sins, but sometimes it takes a while for us to overcome the consequences of bad decisions we have made in the past.

This is actually good, because anyone who is delivered too easily from the results of wrong behavior may find making the same mistakes again and again easy. God is wise and He always does what is right for us, but He also does it at the right time. We may think He is too slow, but His timing in our lives is actually perfect. We may not understand why we have to wait, but there is a reason and God will cause all things to work together for our good as we love and obey Him (Rom. 8:28).

Prayer and Trusting God

I encourage you to pray about your finances on a regular basis, not just when you have a shortage of funds or some pressing financial need. Ask God to bless any investments you may have, to protect your money, to give you good deals, and to bless everything you put your hand to. Trust God at all times for whatever you need in life, and resist the temptation to fear lack.

It is not wrong to pray about money, nor is it wrong to ask God to bless you financially. I spoke to a woman who was fearful of losing her job because she was not meeting the minimum sales quota. She worked in a department store, so I suggested that she pray for God to send customers to her and give her favor with them. She had been a Christian for more than thirty years, so praying was not a new idea to her, but she asked me, "Is it okay to pray for money?" I told her it is. I hope she followed through and still has her job and is the top saleswoman there. I believe she was missing some blessings just because she thought God wasn't concerned about her income. But He is concerned about everything that concerns us, and we should never be afraid to pray and ask Him to help us in any area of life.

Jesus told the disciples to pray: "Give us today our daily bread" (Matt. 6:11). They were to pray for provision for themselves. The Bible has a lot to say about money, including a lot about wealth, greed, contentment, saving, stewardship, and giving. It also talks about remembering that if we seek God first, He will add the other things we desire and need (Matt. 6:33).

> Take delight in the Lord, and he will give you the desires
> of your heart.
>
> Psalm 37:4

The Bible contains about five hundred Scripture verses on prayer and fewer than five hundred on faith, but more than two thousand on finances. God gives us a lot of instruction about money because the way people handle their money says a lot about them.

For example, Jesus said that if we are faithful in little things, we will be made ruler over much (Luke 16:10). If we observe how people handle the little things in their lives, we know ahead of time how they would handle a lot. Some people think that if they had a lot of money they would give more toward God's work. But the truth is that if we won't give a portion of what we have, no matter how little it may be, we wouldn't give if we had more.

God's Word says not to worry about provision, but instead to trust God. He will give you what you need, bless everything you put your hand to, give you success and prosper you (Ps. 1:3; 118:25).

This is one of my absolute favorites of the scriptures that encourage us not to worry about finances:

> [God] Himself has said, I will not in any way fail you nor give you up nor leave you without support. [I will] not, [I will] not, [I will] not in any degree leave you helpless nor forsake nor let [you] down (relax My hold on you)! [Assuredly not!]
>
> Hebrews 13:5 AMPC

My Fears concerning Money

When I was growing up, I had to earn my own money by working. My parents fed, clothed, and housed me, but that was about all. Anything else I wanted I had to do for myself. Even as an adult I never felt I had anyone who would help me financially if I had a need. I worried about not having enough and what would happen to me if I lost my job. I always tried to keep some money saved for emergencies. Although that is a wise way to live, I was extreme about it and had lots of fear connected to my savings. If I had to spend any of what I had set aside, I became fearful.

I always looked for the most economical way to do everything, and I was hesitant to spend money on myself or on anything that wasn't an absolute necessity. My husband, on the other hand, had no fears at all concerning money. He grew up rather poor but had a mother who was filled with faith. Dave saw the Lord provide for them over and over again. Therefore, he had no fear that He would not provide for us.

Dave once told me that my faith was in our little bit of savings, and until I got beyond that, God wouldn't bless us. He was right. I had placed my trust in my bank account, not in God. Whatever money we did have, Dave was never afraid to spend on a valid need and sometimes on something he simply wanted. I envied his freedom concerning finances, but until I actually started "doing it afraid," I stayed in bondage. What I mean is that I had to learn to spend money as well as to save it. We believed in tithing on our income and had done that from the day we married, but we still struggled financially, having only barely enough to get by on until I confronted my fear regarding money.

I am certainly not suggesting that you spend money simply to prove you are not afraid to do so, but I am suggesting that there is no point in God giving us anything if we are going to refuse to use and enjoy it.

Dave has a formula for sound finances. He always says to save some, spend some, and give some within your borders—and God will increase your borders. I agree with him and recommend that you pray about making that strategy part of your life.

I know a young man who is married with two children, and he behaves in a similar way to the way I behaved toward money. His mom was a single mother who received no help from her ex-husband, an alcoholic. Being under financial pressure was the norm for that young man and his mother. His mom did remarry a very kind man, but my friend never got over the lack of finances he experienced during his childhood. Since sitting under my teaching, he has changed some, but admits he still struggles spending money. He would much rather save it than spend it, so in effect, he enjoys very little of what he has, and that is not God's will for us.

The Lord Is My Shepherd, I Shall Not Lack!

You may be familiar with the twenty-third Psalm. Some people have even memorized it and know that it says, "The Lord is my shepherd; I shall not want" (Ps. 23:1 NKJV) The word *want* is a synonym for *lack*. The fear of lack (the fear of not having what you need) is possibly one of the biggest or most frequent fears people deal with. We have an inherent need for preservation and spend a great deal of time trying to make sure that we will be taken care of, as will the people we love.

As children of God, we have the great privilege of trusting Him to take care of us. He tells us over and over that we do not need to worry, but I do realize from personal experience that not worrying is often challenging to do. God does not tell us that we don't need to work; He tells us that we don't need to worry.

There are things we may have to do afraid in order to be free from the fear of lack. Give, even if you have to do it afraid; spend as you're led by the Holy Spirit, even if you have to do it afraid; and turn your worries into prayers. Corrie ten Boom said, "Worry does not empty tomorrow of its sorrow. It empties today of its strength."

Money is not the only thing we can lack. We need wisdom, strength, favor, creativity, and hundreds of other things. At times we can feel we lack those resources, too, but we can trust that God will provide everything we need, not just money. I strongly urge you to be thankful for what you have while waiting for God to give you more. I recall a time when I was complaining in my prayers about how tight our finances were, and God simply spoke to my heart, saying, "Why should I give you

> *Why should God give you more when you are complaining about what you already have?*

more to complain about when you are complaining about what you already have?"

Don't be afraid to ask God for what you want or need, but don't forget to be thankful for what you have. Most of us need to stop and regularly think about how blessed we are, because it is easy to start focusing on what we do not have and to be blind to what we do have.

An Abundant God

I don't believe God's will is for us to live on Barely Get By Street. One of His names in the Old Testament is El Shaddai, meaning "the God of more than enough." I once heard a man teach on "the land of lack, the land of even, and the land of plenty," and I thought it was very enlightening. When you have lived in the land of lack for a long time, you don't go straight from that to the land of plenty; you first must pass through the land of even. That is the place where God provides for you, but not as abundantly as you would like. This land is a testing land, an important place to remain faithful in giving and trusting God to give you abundance at the right time.

"At the right time" is very important. Thankfully, God loves us too much to give us more than we can handle and still keep Him first in our lives. When I pray for provision, I always ask God to bless me, but not to give me more than I can handle and still keep Him first. Things have the ability to draw us away from God, and that is the last thing we should want to happen.

Be Generous

To be generous is to be lavish and abundant. A generous person shares willingly. I think it means doing more than you have to, or being a person who actually watches for opportunities to give and be a blessing to others. I suggest that you ask God to show you who you can bless. This morning I asked God who I could encourage, and right away a woman's name came to my heart, so I called her. We talked a while, and she said it was very encouraging to her that I took time to call her. I just now received a text message from her that says, "You're the best. Your phone call meant the world to me today." All it required from me was a little time, but it meant a great deal to her.

Not all generosity is related to money. It can be expressed simply through listening, reaching out, or helping someone in a practical way. The more generous we are, the less selfish we will be, and one reason Jesus came to earth was so we would no longer live to and for ourselves (2 Cor. 5:15). The most miserable person in the world is the one who is the center of their world. Those people think only of their personal comfort, needs, and desires. They often mistreat others in order to get what they want, and that kind of behavior is not pleasing to God. He wants us to sow good seed by reaching out to others, and then He will bring a harvest into our lives from the good seed we have sown. Stop worrying about how to take care of yourself and let God do it. Do your part and trust God to do what only He can do.

> The most miserable person in the world is the one who is the center of their world.

Stay Out of Debt

One of the best ways to avoid financial pressure is to stay out of debt. Or, if you are already in debt, start right now working toward getting out of it. Being in debt means you have spent your paycheck before you ever got it. If you spend tomorrow's prosperity today, then when tomorrow comes, you will have lack. We must learn to be patient and wait to get things until we have saved the money to purchase them.

There are a few purchases, such as a home or an automobile, for which you may have to take a loan and then spend years making payments, but even an automobile can be purchased with cash if you save a little bit each month toward the next one you will have to buy. If you are making mortgage payments, check into paying a little extra toward the principal of the loan each month, because that will save you a lot of money on interest in the long run.

The Bible encourages us not to owe anyone anything but love (Rom. 13:8). It also says that "The rich rule over the poor, and the borrower is servant to the lender" (Prov. 22:7 AMPC).

Don't let the devil convince you that you could never get out of debt or that it is too late for you. That is exactly what he wants you to think. He wants you to give up before you even try. If you do your best, God will help you, but He won't do everything for you while you continue to waste money or purchase things you should wait to buy. If it has taken you a long time to get into debt, don't expect to get out of it overnight. It may, and probably will, take a long time of working extra hard and waiting on purchases you really want right now, but in the end your diligence will pay off. You will be out of debt and have no worries about lack in your life. Debt creates pressure and anxiety, and I'm sure that you do not want or need either of those, so start reducing your debt today. Even if you can only do it a little bit at a time, if you keep at it and don't give up, you will be financially free.

May your choices reflect your hopes, not your fears.

Nelson Mandela

"Do It Afraid" Sounds Good Until You Have to Do It Yourself

After fourteen years of working in a ministry I absolutely loved, I felt God starting to lead me in a new direction. I can't stress enough that I loved my job and was satisfied in the work I was doing.

As time went on, the initial small feeling went full-blown, and I knew I needed to follow God. It's hard to put into words, but the day I made the decision to follow God *on the inside*, was the same day fear started to cave in all around me *on the outside*.

But rather than lean fully into Him, I continued to lean into fear. And though I'm not proud of it, I started down the path of looking for various reasons why my decision *wasn't* God's. I reminded Him of the following: "You brought me here!" "I work for a ministry!" "My support system is here!"

For me, fear always shows up in the form of questions, such as, "What if I've made this up?" "What if I'm making a huge mistake?" "How will I tell my wife and kids that I'm uprooting our family and moving across the country?"

How did I silence the questions and overcome my fear? Well, it just so happens that the person I was working for was Joyce Meyer. And every time I was working at a conference, she would make statements during her teaching, such as, "God would rather you do something uncomfortable that keeps you in His perfect will than stay comfortable and settle for less." *Okay*, I thought. That got my attention.

We'd have another conference, she'd start teaching and would say, "Making hard decisions is difficult, but if you're asking God for a lot, you better be willing to grow up and do the hard stuff. And if you are simply not sure, you have to step out to find out. And if you have to do it afraid, *do it afraid*. Your feelings change, but God's promise will always sustain you."

"Yes, God, I hear You," I finally said. However, though this helped ease my fears, it did not completely remove them. For that, I had to stay in His Word and turn up the dial on trust. Though I had heard the "do it afraid" message for fourteen years, it was a different story to have to do it myself. It wasn't "Oh, yes, Joyce! People need to learn to do it afraid!" but instead "I have to learn how to do it afraid *for myself.*" In retrospect, what a loss it would have been for me if after all these years of sitting under great teaching, I had found a way to wiggle out of the thing I knew I needed to do. Doing it afraid wasn't one option; it was the *only* option. So I did it!

—Matt

CHAPTER 19

You Can Believe Good Things Are Ahead

Freedom from Fear of the Future

"For I know the plans I have for you," declares the Lord, "plans to prosper you and not to harm you, plans to give you hope and a future."

Jeremiah 29:11

We would all like to know what the future has in store for us. We may have a sense about what our career will be, but concerning the future, God leaves out many details and simply tells us that His plan is for good and not for evil. He has in store for us a future filled with hope.

Fear of the future is one of most frequent fears people have. It is based on fear of the unknown, and we definitely want to know everything that will happen before it happens. The oldest and strongest fear is fear of the unknown. We do not like unsolicited change. We want a nice little plan for our lives, with a chance to preapprove all the details, but we will never have it. Wanting something no one ever has had and no one ever will have is a big waste of

> The oldest and strongest fear is fear of the unknown.

time and emotional energy. God simply says, "Your future will be good. Trust Me!"

Trusting God is one of the Bible's primary themes. The words *faith*, *believe*, and *trust* are seen over and over. These are ways we receive from God, and they help us develop a solid relationship with God that is not shaken even during the most difficult circumstances. They eliminate worry, and that, of course, includes worry about the future. Trust allows us to enjoy the peace that passes understanding. As a matter of fact, trusting God is what allows us to enjoy life. Without it we find no rest for our souls.

We don't even know for sure what will happen in the next five minutes, let alone a year or more from now. God encourages us to trust Him one day at a time. It is easy to talk about trusting God, but doing so is often more difficult.

Some people had great parents who always provided for them and kept them safe, but many of us did not have that childhood foundation of being able to trust. Most of our lives we have had to take care of ourselves. Those who had great parents eventually have to learn to take care of themselves, and it is never easy to let go of something we have come to depend on. Learning to cast our care on God is possibly one of the most difficult things for us to do, but it is the doorway to the good life He intends for us. Without the ability to cast our care, we are always worried about one thing or another, and we are anxious about how things will turn out for us.

After entering into a relationship with God, we begin to learn that He wants us to trust Him and to lean and rely on Him for absolutely everything. This does not mean that we do nothing while God does everything for us, but it does mean that we trust Him more than we trust ourselves or anyone else. We have the privilege of trusting our Lord for protection, provision, strength, and wisdom—and certainly for the future. You can relax, because no matter what your future holds, God knows all about it, and He will go before you and plan your every step.

> The Lord himself goes before you and will be with you; he will never leave you nor forsake you. Do not be afraid; do not be discouraged.
>
> Deuteronomy 31:8

If you were taking your children on a hike in the mountains and you were in territory that required a great deal of caution in order to ensure safety, you would go ahead of your children to make sure the path was safe. We are God's children, and He does the same for us.

The Fear of the Unknown

How would you react if someone said, "I need to talk with you about something, so I'd like to meet with you or set a phone appointment for next week"? Would you look forward to the conversation with enthusiasm, expecting the person to want to talk about something good? Or would you be worried that they were upset with you?

What if your boss left you a message on Monday, saying he wanted to meet with you on Friday at four p.m.? Would your thoughts be filled with faith or with fear? Would you be frightened that you would be let go? Or would you think, *Maybe I'm going to be promoted or get a pay raise!*

Human nature usually pushes us toward the negative unless we reject it and choose to be positive. Look at it like this: You can catch the flu, but you have to choose good health. Satan hurls negative thoughts at us all the time, and we can catch them if we are not careful and watchful, but we can also choose positive thoughts.

Human nature usually pushes us toward the negative unless we reject it and choose to be positive.

In the case of the Friday afternoon meeting, the thoughts you choose would determine what kind of week you would have while waiting to find out what the boss would actually say. This is easier for people with some temperament types than for others. Dave is more patient and easygoing about things than many people are, and he never worries about anything. Waiting a week to know what someone wants to talk to him about would not bother him at all. He wouldn't even think about it until the time came to talk. I, on the other hand, without lots of help from the Holy Spirit, would make myself miserable wondering and trying to reason in my mind what the person might say.

Before knowing Jesus, wondering and reasoning were my only options, but once He came into my life and offered me trust in Him as another option, I started learning to do that. I'm still learning, but I have come a long way.

People so desperately want to know what their futures hold that they spend a lot of money talking with so-called psychics who claim to be able to predict what will happen. According to IBISWorld.com, there are about ninety-four thousand businesses that offer these services, and they bring in a whopping estimated $2 billion a year.

I wish people would give me that kind of money for telling them their future! It's the same message for everyone: Believe in God, and your future will be good. That might be challenging at times, but life with God is still the best option available. It is sad when people are willing to spend so much money to talk with someone who claims to be able to predict the future when we can talk with God for free.

God forbids the seeking of mediums or witches and any type of fortune-telling. He is actually offended when we turn to these means to find out about the future, because no one knows the future except Him.

> Do not turn to mediums or seek out spiritists, for you will be defiled by them. I am the Lord your God.
>
> Leviticus 19:31

> Let no one be found among you who sacrifices their son or daughter in the fire, who practices divination or sorcery, interprets omens, engages in witchcraft, or casts spells, or who is a medium or spiritist or who consults the dead. Anyone who does these things is detestable to the Lord; because of these same detestable practices the Lord your God will drive out those nations before you. You must be blameless before the Lord your God. The nations you will dispossess listen to those who practice sorcery or divination. But as for you, the Lord your God has not permitted you to do so.
>
> Deuteronomy 18:10–14

Many Christians seek the services of fortune-tellers or psychics, not realizing that God has forbidden it. I once worked with a girl who wouldn't make an appointment to get her hair cut without consulting the stars to see which time of the month would be favorable for a haircut. She had begun talking with me quite frequently about astrology charts and zodiac signs, and it was intriguing to my reasoning. At the time, I was a Christian, but because I was not fully committed to God, I felt something was missing. The devil was waiting for an opportunity to try to satisfy that hunger with something that would poison my life, such as astrology. Thankfully, before he got a chance to use her to pull me into something that was not good, God touched my life and brought me into a deeper relationship with Him.

The Bible does say that there will be signs in the sun, moon, and stars prior to Jesus' second coming (Luke 21:25). The stars are beautiful, and they certainly have a function in God's creation, but we are not to look to them for advice or knowledge about the future. People who are into astrology may ask you what sign you are born under, and my answer to that question is "the Cross." That's a good time to tell someone that you get your advice from God and that they can, too.

Yes, people will go to great lengths to try to find out what the future holds, but it is probably good that God hides it from us, because if we knew everything that was going to happen throughout our lives, I think life might be boring. It seems that God loves a good mystery, and most of us do, too. We don't have to search for one because our future is the biggest mystery of all. It unfolds daily and holds many surprises. Yes, there will be disappointing and painful situations, but if we trust God, He will take those things and mix them with all the good things, causing them to work out for one big, combined blessing in our lives.

Though I was sexually abused by my father and abandoned by my mother, God healed my wounded soul and now allows me to use my past to help others who have been hurt. My first husband was unfaithful, a liar, and a thief, but after him came Dave, who has been my wonderful husband for more than fifty-three years.

If you are hurting right now or have suffered an injustice, you can expect God to bring something good to follow your pain.

I think fear is behind the obsession with knowing the future. More than anything else, most of us are curious about it because we want to try to avoid being hurt or unhappy.

Our pain shouts, "It is all too much! Life is too miserable to bear!" But God shouts even louder, "I am here and I have a good plan for your life, so don't give up!"

I know from experience that somewhere in the midst of our suffering we must begin to believe that something good is going to happen. When we do, it opens the door for God to step in with His amazing power.

Get Comfortable Not Knowing

God worked with me for a long time as He taught me how to be comfortable not knowing what was going to happen and when it was going to happen. The apostle Paul said:

> For I resolved to know nothing while I was with you except Jesus Christ and him crucified.
>
> 1 Corinthians 2:2

Did Paul perhaps have a problem with wanting to know things God wasn't telling him yet? Paul was a very intelligent and well-educated man, so it is not too much of a stretch to surmise that he may have been a thinker. Those of us who are thinkers can easily spend too much time thinking about things we should simply trust God to take care of or guide us to take care of them.

I was working on this book just after having lunch with a woman who knew nothing about what I was writing, and I asked her what kinds of things caused her to feel stressed. She said right away, "The fear of the unknown." Then I told her I was currently writing a book on fear and was in the middle of a chapter on fear of the future. She said that thoughts of retirement and financial concerns leave her uneasy. She is single and needs to help two members of her family financially. She helps one because of old age and another because of some mental challenges. Her job income fluctuates because it is seasonal, and she is never sure how much she will make. She has no one to depend on but God and said she has to keep talking to the Father (God) about these situations in order to stay calm.

I like that she keeps talking to the Father until she calms down. Thankfully, we all have Him to talk to. He is our Comforter and gives better advice than anyone else. We don't need to know the future as long as we know the One who does know it.

> We don't need to know the future as long as we know the One who does know it.

People experience different fears based on their particular life situations. A single person deals with fears that a married person doesn't. A parent feels fears that someone without children does not. We all have the same opportunity to trust God and do it afraid, no matter what our unique situation may be. We should keep going forward even if our knees shake occasionally and we get some butterflies in our stomachs.

I was once a very nosy person who wanted to know everyone's business and what was going on in every situation at work, at church, in the neighborhood, at my children's school, and in other places. But now I only want to know what I need to know in order to do what I am supposed to do. The rest of it only overloads my mind and irritates my soul. I look forward to the future, but when I think about it, I will admit it is a total mystery. Even if we think we have it all figured out, we don't. God is full of surprises. At different times in my life, I have been an abused teenager, a divorcée with a child, a waitress, a credit manager, an office clerk, a stay-at-home mom, and a married woman with four children, but I ended up in ministry teaching God's Word and authoring more than one hundred books. Back when I was a waitress, I would have never imagined my future to be what I am doing now, not even in my wildest fantasy! Believe me, your future will be much better than you could imagine if you stay on board with God and let Him take the lead.

Sure, fear will rear its ugly head frequently, but all you need to remember is that God is with you and you can do it, even if you have to do it afraid!

But now having seen him which is invisible I fear not what man can do unto me.

Anne Hutchinson

Don't Be Afraid to Step Out

Fear was common in the atmosphere at my seventeen-year corporate job because layoffs occurred every few years. I thought of leaving many times, but I was too afraid to make a change.

As the years went by, I became restless. I was uninterested in and unfulfilled by the work I was doing. My job no longer "fit" me, and a nagging question grew in my heart: *God, what do You want me to do with my life?*

He gave me clear instruction to leave the company and opened the door wide. I had to make the decision to walk through it. Was I afraid? You bet! I was terrified to go into the abyss of the unknown: *What kind of job was I to look for? What if I didn't find a job soon? What about the bills?*

After all, God never said *when* my new opportunity would come or *what* it would be; He simply said, "Trust Me."

During that fear-filled waiting time, I discovered Joyce Meyer's television program and watched her daily. When she said many times we must "do it afraid," I felt empowered with a new mindset. God was changing me, and fear was being pruned from my personality.

After three years and ten months (I was counting), God led me out of the waiting room to my new opportunity—six states and eleven hours away from my hometown. Before, I'd been fearful of traveling to job interview sites much closer to home than that. This time, I was supernaturally *unafraid*.

I found that the bigger I let God be in my life, the smaller my fear became, until it was gone. Instead, the day I packed my car and drove away, I was filled with excitement, not fear, at the newness, hope, and expectancy of this adventure.

I was doing it, and no longer afraid!

—Rebecca

CHAPTER 20

You Can Trust God in Every Situation

Freedom from the Fear That Bad Things Will Happen

And call on me in the day of trouble; I will deliver you, and you will honor me.

Psalm 50:15

The word *trouble* covers a variety of unpleasant situations. It can mean we are experiencing difficulty, inconvenience, worry, anxiety, distress, concern, disquiet, unease, irritation, vexation, or annoyance. It also refers to something that causes alarm, distress, or torment. These are all things we do not want and try to avoid, but we never do, at least not entirely.

Jesus told us that in the world we would have trouble, and His advice was for us to cheer up because He has overcome the world (John 16:33). He also said that He was leaving us His own special peace, not a type of peace the world offers, but *His* peace! He added, "Do not let your hearts be troubled" (John 14:27). In the world, if people get everything the way they want it and all their circumstances are good, then they believe they have peace, but the peace of God is entirely different. It is available to us when nothing is going the way we want it to go and when we encounter trouble, trials, and tribulation.

Paul wrote to Timothy that trouble would increase in the last days. He was very specific and mentioned many situations we experience today—people becoming "lovers of themselves, lovers of money, boastful, proud, abusive, disobedient to their parents, ungrateful, unholy, without love, unforgiving, slanderous, without self-control, brutal, not lovers of the good, treacherous, rash, conceited, lovers of pleasure rather than lovers of God" (2 Tim. 3:2–4). Today we experience all of these to a greater degree than in previous years, and many people are frightened because of the times in which we live. The Bible even says that in these times people's hearts will fail them because of fear (Luke 21:26 NKJV).

When Jesus warns us of trouble ahead of time, I believe He does it not so we will not be afraid, but so we can be prepared. Those who believe in Jesus have no need to fear, because in addition to giving us warnings of how difficult the end times will be, He has also promised to take care of us and to not allow us to be tempted beyond what we can bear (1 Cor. 10:13).

I can understand how nonbelievers would live in fear, because today we hear regular reports of people simply going shopping and being randomly shot while they are out. In the past few years, we have had mass shootings at schools, colleges, movie theaters, concerts, shopping malls, a nightclub, several churches, an office party, a military base, a naval yard, and other ordinary places. Most of the people killed were not targeted because of anything they did. They were simply killed or injured because of where they were when the shooter started shooting. In addition, we have had terrorist attacks, one of the worst being the 9/11 attack on the twin towers of New York City's World Trade Center and the Pentagon, in which 2,996 people were killed.

The world is full of strife, bickering, arguing, and hatred. I could write on and on about how terrible conditions are in the world, but I would rather convince you that no matter how bad it gets, you don't have to live in fear. We should use wisdom, be cautious, pay attention to what is going on around us, lock our doors, not leave small children unattended in public places, and use common sense, but once again, let me say that we don't have to live afraid.

I Will Fear No Evil

Fear is a dead end, but faith always has a future. Fear sees no way out, but faith believes that God will make a way. The psalmist David said, "I will fear no evil" (Ps. 23:4). God's definition of evil, according to the Christian view, is any action, thought, or attitude that is contrary to the character or will of God.

> *Fear is a dead end, but faith always has a future.*

Satan is the evil one (Matt. 13:19), and all his works are evil, but we don't need to fear because God will direct us and help us live peaceful, enjoyable lives in the midst of turmoil and trouble.

> But whoso hearkens to me [Wisdom] shall dwell securely and in confident trust and shall be quiet, without fear or dread of evil.
>
> Proverbs 1:33 AMPC

Biblical history tells of many times when God protected His people, even though disaster and evil engulfed the wicked. In Sodom and Gomorrah, He sent angels to warn Lot and his family to leave the city before it was destroyed (Gen. 19:12–16). When

God brought a flood that destroyed the whole earth, He saved Noah and his family because they were righteous (Gen. 7:1–5). When God brought ten plagues on Egypt because of their wickedness, the Bible says that God protected His people who lived in a place called Goshen (Exod. 8, 9).

There is no reason for us to believe God won't also protect those of us who believe in Him from the evils of the end times. This doesn't mean that we won't experience trouble, trials, and tribulations, but God will protect us. In Mark 4, Jesus corrected the disciples because they were afraid of a storm raging around them. He wanted them to trust Him.

At one point during his ministry, Paul said that a wide door of opportunity had opened to him and with it came many adversaries (1 Cor. 16:9). Satan uses trouble in the hopes of getting us to back down from the opportunities God gives us, but we should always stand firm and not shrink back in fear (Heb. 10:39).

The apostle James told us we should remain patient in the midst of various trials and tribulations (James 1:2–3). Patience is a fruit of the Spirit that grows only under trial. Not even a small muscle in the human body can get bigger or grow stronger without resistance. Our faith is like a muscle; it must be exercised in order to grow.

Our Faith Is Tested

I don't know what you may be going through at this time in your life. Perhaps it is a very good time, but it may be very difficult or even tragic. Perhaps a loved one has died, or you have lost your job with all your retirement and insurance benefits. You might be sick or in pain, you could be dealing with depression, or perhaps you are facing the challenges of caring for elderly parents.

Trusting God is easy when we have no problems, but trusting Him when we find ourselves struggling is quite different. It is something we must choose to do, perhaps several times a day.

Satan paints in our imaginations an unpleasant picture of all the terrible things that could happen, but we can look away from his distractions to Jesus, who has promised to never leave us and who is our Comforter (2 Cor. 1:3–4) and our Strength.

The Word of God tells us repeatedly that our faith will be tested:

> Dear friends, do not be surprised at the fiery ordeal that has come on you to test you, as though something strange were happening to you.
>
> 1 Peter 4:12

> In all this you greatly rejoice, though now for a little while you may have had to suffer grief in all kinds of trials. These have come so that the proven genuineness of your faith—of greater worth than gold, which perishes even though refined by fire—may result in praise, glory and honor when Jesus Christ is revealed.
>
> 1 Peter 1:6–7

These verses basically tell us that fiery trials will test our faith. That doesn't sound pleasant, but believe it or not, it does have an upside. If we go through the trials and don't give up on God, we grow spiritually, and our faith that has been tested and tried becomes stronger than it was previously.

Set Your Mind

Although we know we will face times of difficulty, we are to set our minds to believe that when those hardships come, we will be strong through Christ, and that with His help, we will stand firm in faith. Being committed and mentally prepared to go all the way through with God will make it easier to do it when the time comes.

Dave *loves* to play golf. I asked him how he thought he would do if he ever got to the point where he couldn't play any longer, and he said, "I've already thought about that, and I have set my mind that I could enjoy my life anyway."

He had migraine headaches when he was younger, and he always dreaded them because of the way they made him feel and the pain they caused. But God spoke to his heart to not be impressed by the headaches, because he could still enjoy his life. He acted on that, and when a headache would begin he would say, "I'm not impressed," and the headaches stopped completely.

If what Satan is doing to us does not affect us negatively, then he will stop and wait for another opportunity.

In times of trouble, you can renew your mind by meditating on and declaring God's Word. I challenge you: For the next thirty days, a few times each day, declare the words of the apostle Paul:

> I have strength for all things in Christ Who empowers me [I am ready for anything and equal to anything through Him Who infuses inner strength into me; I am self-sufficient in Christ's sufficiency].
>
> Philippians 4:13 AMPC

Doing this will help you set your mind in the right direction and prepare you for victory before you need it.

We are more than conquerors through Christ (Rom. 8:37), and if we truly believe that, then we don't need to fear evil. When we do face a troubling time, we know that when it comes, it is temporary, and that God, who loves us, will actually work it out for good in our lives (Rom. 8:28).

People have even said that having a life-threatening disease changed their lives in a positive way because it made them realize what was truly important. When they recovered, they were changed for the better.

If you have a problem so big that no one can help you but God, it will cause you to seek Him like never before. I've heard that we don't qualify for a miracle until our problem is so big that only God can fix it.

All of our tests and trials are not life-threatening. Many are merely annoying or aggravating, but God uses them to stretch our faith or help us grow in patience. The reason for this may be so we can have more compassion for others who are hurting, but whatever it is, if we keep a good attitude and continue trusting God, He will make sure it benefits us in the long run. What our enemy means for harm, God intends for good (Gen. 50:20).

> *We don't qualify for a miracle until our problem is so big that only God can fix it.*

Painfully Wonderful

I believe I can say, like many of you, that my life has been painful. I have dealt with sexual abuse, divorce, a miscarriage, breast cancer, two hip replacements, a minor back surgery, bunion surgery, rejection, abandonment, criticism, and unfair judgment. I've battled fear, doubt, anxiety, reasoning, jealousy, insecurity, anger, and bitterness—and that's just the beginning of a list that could be quite lengthy. Yes, it has been painful, but at the same time wonderful. If I look at my life as a whole, I have to say it has been awesome! Amazing! Wonderful! Would I want to go back and erase all the pain? I would have to say no, because I don't think I would appreciate the good things in my life the way I do without having experienced the pain.

Even the sexual abuse in my childhood, as horrific and evil as it was, has helped make me the person I am today. I don't believe for one second that God designed that terrible experience for my good, but He has worked good things out of it.

The way our pain impacts us depends in part on our attitude. I know you have probably heard the statement "You can be bitter or better," and it really is true. Your attitude belongs to you, and it is one thing nobody controls but you.

I've met people who have had very minor trials and have allowed themselves to become bitter and filled with self-pity, and I have met others who have had tragic things happen to them but have remained kind and helpful to others. They don't complain. In fact, they seem to be some of the most thankful people I know.

They had a choice, and they made a good one, a choice that would allow them to get the most out of life and to use their pain for their gain and for the gain of others. They practiced letting go of the things behind them and pressing toward the things ahead.

Perhaps you are reading this book right now and recognize the need for an attitude adjustment in your life. If so, just choose to make that adjustment and ask God to help you. Be persistent day after day and refuse to give up until you get the full victory. Take the lemons life has handed you and make a lemon pie with lots of whipped cream on top! You can beat the devil at his own game if you learn to play according to God's rules. Don't get upset or worry about people who try to do evil, but trust in the Lord and keep doing good (Ps. 37:1–3).

Philippians 1:28 is a wonderful scripture that clearly shows us how God wants us to respond to the devil's tactics:

> And do not [for a moment] be frightened or intimidated in anything by your opponents and adversaries, for such [constancy and fearlessness] will be a clear sign (proof and seal) to them of [their impending] destruction, but [a sure token and evidence] of your deliverance and salvation, and that from God. (AMPC)

This verse helped me greatly, and I believe that if you will study it, thinking about the words and what they are really saying, it will help you, too. It teaches us that being constant and fearless when the enemy attacks us is a clear sign to him of his impending destruction. To God, it is a sure token and evidence of our upcoming deliverance. In other words, the devil sees he cannot control you, and God sees that your trust is in Him and delivers you.

It Won't Last Forever

Whatever problem you might be facing now, it won't last forever. Just think of the other things you have gone through in life, and yet you are still here. Those problems are gone, and you are probably wiser and stronger than you were previously.

The fear of upcoming problems is actually worse than going through them. You might fear something for years and get through it in two months. A pregnant woman once told me she was afraid that when the time came for her baby to be born, it would hurt. I told her she didn't need to fear that anymore, because it would definitely hurt, but she would get through it and forget the pain as soon as she held her beautiful child. Sure enough, she made it through and even did it again. There is no point in fearing what is inevitable. If you decide you want to be a doctor, you can't avoid the many years of school and the years of residency you will need to endure, but once they are over, you will be a doctor for the rest of your life.

Be willing to go through whatever you need to go through in order to become what you truly want to be or to have what you really want to have. If you need to lose weight, you can do it, but you will probably be hungry at least for a while until your stomach shrinks back to a normal size. Our addiction to comfort often keeps us from the freedom and breakthroughs that we need. Perhaps we need to toughen up a bit and not expect everything in life to be easy. We are anointed with God's power, and that means we can do whatever we need to do in life and do it with a good attitude, fearing nothing.

> Our addiction to comfort often keeps us from the freedom and breakthroughs that we need.

First of all, let me assert my firm belief that the only thing we have to fear is fear itself—nameless, unreasoning, unjustified terror which paralyzes needed efforts to convert retreat into advance.

Franklin D. Roosevelt

Who's Going to Protect My Family?

One of my biggest fears is not being prepared enough for a major disaster. Or not prepared enough if an intruder comes into my home. I have always been a planner, so I worry about all the things that could happen.

I wouldn't label myself a "prepper," because I don't have gallons of water stashed in my basement next to a year's supply of freeze-dried food. But I try to make sure my bases are covered.

Over the years, I've discovered that my fear is rooted in the pressure to protect and provide for my family. As a man, I carry the responsibility that their safety is in my hands. And that thought is overwhelming. It means providing for them financially with a stable job. It means providing for them emotionally by being a present husband and dad. It means providing safety and security both inside and outside our home.

As a Christian, I've always been taught to trust God in everything, that He is our provider. I say that I trust Him and that I believe He will always provide, and I truly do mean that. But, my thoughts and actions sometimes prove otherwise. So, how do I find balance between truly trusting God to supply all my needs, including in a disaster situation or with the protection of my family, but also use the wisdom God gives me to prepare in a logical way?

If I'm not careful I can drive myself crazy with worry and fear and let my thoughts get away from me. I can get so worked up in my mind about these things that my stomach will start to ache. The fear can make me feel physically ill.

But I've come to the realization that I can't control everything. I can't be with my wife and kids 24/7 to keep them safe. I may not even always be around to provide for them financially. But God can. He is a big God. I need to give Him a little more credit than I do. He knows my heart, and He knows I am doing my best. I don't need to fear not doing enough, because He's got it all covered.

—Mike

CHAPTER 21

You Can Relax

Freedom from the Fear of Not Doing Enough

For it is by grace you have been saved, through faith—and this is not from yourselves, it is the gift of God—not by works, so that no one can boast.

Ephesians 2:8–9

We conducted a survey in our office and asked people what they would want to ask Jesus if they could sit down with Him for a while. The number one question turned out to be "How can I know when I'm doing enough?" I knew I had suffered with this haunting question, but I had no idea that so many other people had, too. I assumed my addiction to "doing" came from insecurities that stemmed from being abused sexually by my father. I think I felt for many years that I had to prove my worth and value, but thankfully, the truth found in God's Word has set me free from that. However, I readily admit that I still have twinges of feeling that perhaps I haven't worked enough on any given day.

After my hip replacement surgery, my daughter stayed with me for a few days. She and Dave were trying to take care of me, but I wanted to *do something*. My daughter asked me, "Why can't you just be still?"

I replied that I didn't want to get lazy. She looked at me rather oddly, and then began to laugh hysterically. She said, "If anyone is in danger of getting lazy, it isn't *you!*" She said that because she knows I always want to be sure I am doing enough.

I am a very responsible person, and some of my desire to make sure I am doing enough may have come from that, but more of it was rooted in the fear that God would not be pleased with me if I didn't do enough. That fear came from my father, who placed no value on having fun and seemed to be pleased with me only when I was working. I can actually remember getting in trouble for laughing. My father was a very unhappy man, and it seemed to annoy him if anyone around him was happy.

Perhaps you also struggle with the fear of not doing enough, but you did not have an abusive childhood. As a matter of fact, it was just the opposite. Your parents were great; you knew you were loved; you excelled in school and had other positive experiences. So you might wonder, "Why am I like this? Why is it hard for me to rest without feeling guilty?" I think our society gives us the impression that the harder we work and the more we own, the more valuable we are. Although this isn't true, if we even subconsciously believe that it is, that belief will influence us negatively.

> *Why is it hard for me to rest without feeling guilty?*

God Redeems Us

God redeems everything the devil has stolen from us. For Christians, the word *redeem* means that Jesus purchased our freedom with the price of His blood, which was poured out for our redemption. He has restored to me many things that were stolen in my childhood and through other dysfunctional relationships. One of them is the freedom from always being afraid I'm not doing enough.

If you wrestle with that same fear, He wants to do the same for you. It is for freedom that Christ has set us free (Gal. 5:1). Any kind of fear is bondage, and God wants to set us free from it. We cannot be set free from something we don't recognize as a problem. It is possible that some people—maybe even you— have had a particular fear most of your life without ever realizing you shouldn't feel the way it makes you feel. You don't have to be afraid you are not doing enough, because no matter how much you do, it can never be enough. That is why Jesus did all that was needed and no more sacrifice is required. Always remember that Jesus' sacrifice was a perfect one, and we never need to add anything else to it. No amount of "doing" will make God love you any more than He does right now.

This understanding helped me realize why I usually lived with a low-level guilty feeling if I was resting or watching television. God showed me that I felt guilty because I didn't think I deserved to enjoy myself unless all my work was done. The problem with that kind of wrong thinking is that no matter how much we do, there is always more to be done. We must do our best each day and then get the rest and enjoyment we need to be refreshed so we can begin again the next day.

Obviously, this doesn't mean that we shouldn't discipline ourselves to do the work we need to do, or that it's permissible to be lazy and unproductive. Work is important, but rest is just as important as work.

Made Acceptable

We are made acceptable to God through our faith in Jesus Christ. Therefore, we do not have to do a certain amount of work or make a certain number of sacrifices in order for Him to accept us.

Working to earn acceptance may be the world's standard, but it is not God's.

We no longer need to ask: *Did I pray long enough? Did I read the Bible long enough? Did I watch television too much? Am I giving enough? Was I kind enough to other people?* Our minds can be filled with "Am I enough?" questions, and the answer to each of them is "Yes, I am enough through Jesus, who died for me and has risen from the dead." If God convicts us that we need to do something, then by all means we should do it promptly, remembering that we obey Him because we love Him and not to earn anything from Him. The Holy Spirit will let us know when we need to work more, study more, or do more of something else, but He also wants to let us know when we need to lay work aside and rest and enjoy ourselves.

Wondering if God may be disappointed or perhaps even angry with us represents a type of fear. It is one of the most oppressing types of fear because it never allows us to rest without feeling guilty. If you had three children and each morning they came to you and asked, "What can we do for you today to get you to accept us?" you would probably be offended that they didn't believe you loved them without their doing something to deserve it. If our children do something for us, we want them to do so because they truly want to, not because they think they have to in order to buy our love with their good works.

We want our prayers to be answered, but they are not answered due to our perfection. When we pray in Jesus' name, we are presenting to God all that Jesus is, not all that we are. Otherwise, we would pray in our own names.

> And I will do [I Myself will grant] whatever you ask in My Name [as presenting all that I Am], so that the Father may be glorified and extolled in (through) the Son.

[Yes] I will grant [I Myself will do for you] whatever
you shall ask in My Name [as presenting all that I Am].

John 14:13–14 AMPC

Jesus Invites the Weary to Come to Him

Jesus said that when we are weary, heavy-laden, or overburdened, we should come to Him and He will give us rest (Matt. 11:28). Please notice that He didn't say, "Come to Me and I will give you a list of things to do." When we are weary, Jesus wants us to enter His rest, which is a kind of rest that refreshes us mentally, emotionally, physically, and spiritually. It is a complete rest. We need it, and God wants us to have it.

In Matthew 11:29, Jesus said for us to take His yoke on us and learn how He does things. Jesus didn't just rest *from* work, He rested *while* He worked, and we can learn to do the same. If we study the word *rest* in its original New Testament Greek language, we learn that it was initially translated as resting "from" something. Actually, it is not just a rest from work, but an invitation to learn how to do what we do in faith and rest rather than in fear and weariness.

When Jesus ascended into heaven, He sent the Holy Spirit to earth to help us. He wants to be invited to help us with everything we do. If we are doing the will of God, the Holy Spirit gives us grace to do it, and that allows us to accomplish it with a holy ease. It is when we frantically try to do things by ourselves while being afraid we are not doing enough that we labor and feel overburdened. But even if that describes where you are right now in your life, you have an invitation to "come to Jesus" and learn how to enter His unique rest.

All the requirements of God have been met in Jesus Christ. He came to earth and took on human flesh in order to do for us what we could never do for ourselves. What He asks in return is that we believe in Him, put our faith and trust in Him, and simply obey Him as a proof of our trust. If we understand and believe

> *All the requirements of God have been met in Jesus Christ.*

that what Jesus did for us was done out of His love, not because of our works, then we can do the works with joy and a holy ease. And we can do them because we love Jesus.

Work Done from a Pure Heart

The only work we do that is acceptable to God is work that is done with a pure heart. Practically speaking, what does that mean?

1. Work done for God must be done purely because we love Him.
2. Work done for God must be done in obedience to Him and His Word.
3. Work done for God must be done in faith, leaning entirely on Him for its success.
4. Work done for God must not be done to be seen and approved of by people, or to get their applause, admiration, or acknowledgment. Purity of motive is God's desire, and it should be ours, also.

The Bible teaches us that when we stand before God for our works to be judged, they will pass through the fire, and only the ones that are pure will be rewarded. The rest will be burned up, and we will not have the reward we would have had if they had been pure. We will be saved but lose any reward we might have enjoyed (1 Cor. 3:12–15).

I love the Lord, and I want my rewards when I get to heaven. This is why I make an effort to examine my heart and always be sure that my motives for the work I do for the Lord are pure. Sometimes we deceive ourselves and don't truly know our own hearts, so I depend on God to reveal to me any impure motives I may have.

The psalmist David invited God to examine his heart and see if there was any wicked way in him (Ps. 139:23–24). We would be wise to follow that example, because God knows more about our hearts than we do. We never have to be *condemned* (Rom. 8:1), but we do need to receive the *conviction* of the Holy Spirit regarding behavior that is not pleasing to Him. Conviction is not negative; it is positive. To me, it is God's way of showing His love to me and keeping me out of trouble.

When we pray, give, study God's Word, or do any kind of good works, we should not approach them hoping to gain approval from God. We already have His approval because we believe in Him. Since He sent His Son to die for us while we were still dead in our sin (Col. 2:13–14; Rom. 5:8), I think it is evident that He loves us unconditionally and His love is not at all based on any good work we do.

Don't Be So Hard on Yourself

The world and the devil are hard enough on us. We don't need to assist them by being excessively hard on ourselves. God is merciful! When we receive His mercy, it enables us to be merciful toward ourselves. I found early in my walk with God that the reason I struggled to be merciful toward others was that I wasn't receiving God's mercy for myself. I often say, "We cannot give away what we don't have." Receive God's mercy for your own sins, mistakes, and failures, and you will find it easy to be merciful toward the weaknesses of others.

We all have weaknesses, and Jesus understands them because He was tempted, just as we are. The difference is that He did not sin (Heb. 4:15). Weakness is totally different from wickedness. No born-again believer is wicked because the nature of God is in them. His heart and Spirit have taken up residence inside of their spirit, and they cannot continue habitually and knowingly in sin (1 John 3:9). We all display weakness at times. We all sin and miss God's mark at times, but that is totally different from being wicked and living in purposeful, habitual sin.

People with special needs children don't expect or demand from them what they might from children without the same limitations. Likewise, God knows us, and we are all human beings with inbred weaknesses. Although we are in the process of being changed from glory to glory into the image of Jesus Christ (2 Cor. 3:18), He knows we have not arrived yet. Jesus is a merciful high priest who understands our weakness and infirmities, and He wants us to have that same attitude of mercy and compassion toward the people we deal with in our lives.

I call fear "Satan's tool of torment." When we succumb to fear, it steals the joy from everything we do. Fear torments because it threatens punishment, but the apostle John, inspired by the Holy Spirit, wrote, "There is no fear in love. But perfect love drives out fear" (1 John 4:18). God is the only One who can love us perfectly and unconditionally, and it is His love that drives fear out of our hearts. When we know that He accepts us completely, the fear that we are not enough vanishes from our lives.

I believe we open a door for all kinds of trouble if we refuse to believe that God is pleased with us because of our faith in Jesus and that alone. Two different times during Jesus' three-year ministry on earth, a voice came from heaven, saying, "This is my beloved Son, with whom I am well pleased" (Matt. 3:17; 17:5 ESV). Jesus received the words of His Father. He didn't reject them. Had He done so, it would have caused many problems. We need to believe that God loves and approves of us. Of course, He is not pleased with all of our behavior, because we are still growing spiritually, but He is pleased with us as individuals who love Him and want to do what is right.

I strongly recommend that you believe and say quietly in your heart, "God is pleased with me." You can even go a step further and speak it out loud when you are alone. That will help give you confidence and set you free from the fear that you are not doing enough.

Have enough courage to trust love one more time, and always one more time.

Maya Angelou

The Fear of Intimacy because of Past Pain

Whether it's with a new friendship or with relationship commitment issues, fear continues to show up and keep me from real connection. And though the relationships start with excitement and joy, my mind always messes with me, leaving me with anxiety, doubt, and distrust.

During my teenage years, my parents went through a tough season when my mother discovered my father was cheating on her. This breakdown within our small family also led to changes in relationships with other relatives and close family friends. As reality set in that the dynamics of the family were not what they used to be, many ugly truths started to pop up.

As a family, we spoke honestly about how we felt. This was predominately because my mother pushed those conversations. My father took a more reflective, quiet, backseat role—many of the character traits I find in myself today.

I regularly found myself talking to my mother about those issues, but never my father, as though silence or a different topic of conversation were a better path to take. This led to a number of unanswered questions, some of which remain unanswered today.

And as I have grown, it's become very clear to me that I don't want to end up like my father, and this is the root of my fear when it comes to relationships. I want to be committed to the various relationships in my life, but this fear has been the major roadblock to getting there.

I would love nothing more than answers from my dad so I can avoid his mistakes; yet I see the pain and scarring it has left. But the idea of bringing these feelings up to my dad terrifies me.

I know this is something I will have to commit to Jesus. I will have to choose freedom over fear and ask Him for His wisdom and courage—to have the boldness to get past this fear that keeps me from long-lasting relationships.

—Ashley

CHAPTER 22

You Can Build Healthy Relationships

Freedom from the Fear of Trusting God and Others

You will keep in perfect peace those whose minds are steadfast, because they trust in you.

Isaiah 26:3

Fearful people cannot trust. They live in agony because they continually try to take care of themselves, endeavoring to make sure they are safe and trying not to allow others to take advantage of them. People who have been hurt, abused, betrayed, or abandoned are especially prone to this fear. The memories of pain from their past cause them to live in a self-protective mode, which never allows them to simply trust, relax, and enjoy life.

None of us has a guarantee that we will never be hurt or disappointed. We do, however, have the promise that if we put our trust in God, He will judge righteously and always be our vindicator.

We need to develop an intimate, trusting relationship with God before we can do the same with people. Many scriptures instruct us to trust God, and although that sounds easy, we often find it difficult. Trust requires that we have some unanswered questions in our lives and demands that we become comfortable with not knowing how or when God will do what we need Him to do. We are to cast our care on Him and believe that He will care for us (1 Pet. 5:7).

We are created for connectedness, not aloneness. But if we are continually afraid we will be taken advantage of, we withdraw from intimacy and prefer a comfortable distance between ourselves and other people. We might have some relationships, but we make sure they are kept at a distance that feels safe to us. We may let people in, but never enough to be truly close or intimate.

> *We are created for connectedness, not aloneness.*

Intimacy with God

Jesus didn't die so we could have our preferred brand of religion, but so we might have a close, intimate, personal relationship with God through Him. When Jesus came to earth clothed in human flesh, He developed close relationships with a variety of people, but He could only do that because He had a close relationship with His heavenly Father.

God has already come close to us in Christ, and we are invited to come close to Him:

> Come near to God and he will come near to you.
>
> James 4:8

We can open our entire lives to Him without fear of being rejected. He already knows everything there is to know about us. He knows what we are going to do and say before we do it. One way we can develop closeness with God is by talking with Him about absolutely everything, holding nothing back. We can't keep secrets from God anyway, so why keep trying to do so?

You can talk to God and hear Him talk to you. He speaks in a variety of ways, but you can learn to recognize His voice. Jesus said that those who are His know His voice (John 10:3–4).

The apostle Paul said that his "determined purpose" was to know God and to come to know the power of His resurrection (Phil. 3:10 AMPC). He didn't just want to know *about* God; he wanted to *know* God. Many people know about God. They have heard of Him and may even believe He exists, but they have not received Him into their hearts and trusted Him for everything that concerns them.

An intimate, trusting relationship with God is what sets us free from many tormenting fears and behavior patterns. In the context of that kind of relationship, we can retire from trying to take care of everything ourselves and begin to experience life the way God intended us to live it.

Nobody knows how to take care of us like God does, and He wants to be invited to do so. Jesus always trusted His Father to take care of Him. Even when He was being mistreated and falsely accused, He put His trust in Father God:

> When they hurled their insults at him, he did not retaliate; when he suffered, he made no threats. Instead, he entrusted himself to him who judges justly.
>
> 1 Peter 2:23

Just imagine the joy and freedom of no longer feeling the need to take care of and protect yourself all the time for fear of being hurt or taken advantage of. How much easier would life be if you never thought about how to get someone back when they have hurt you? Think about how free you would feel if you never felt compelled to make sure they did not hurt you again because you trust God to bring justice in His perfect timing.

I recall a group of ladies who once hurt me deeply. Ten years passed before they apologized, but they finally did. I remember well what the spokesperson for the group said to me: "God showed us that we were wrong in what we said about you and did to you, and we are sorry." God gave me justice. Perhaps not as quickly as I would have preferred, but while I was waiting He taught me many valuable lessons about forgiveness, praying for our enemies, and loving people who are not easy to love.

I've seen God's vindication many times in my life, and I believe I will continue to do so. You may have seen the same, but if not, you can begin today trusting God rather than trying to do it all yourself.

Can We Really Trust God?

We can definitely trust God! He may not always give us what we want, but if He doesn't, it is because He has something better in mind for us. We are usually in a hurry, but God is not, and His timing will be perfect. He would rather do quality work in us and in our lives rather than a quick one.

> We are usually in a hurry, but God is not.

We may wonder if God will take care of us or not, and the only way to find out is to give it a try. I know by experience and by the Word of God that He can be trusted, but it took me quite a while to be willing to cease my own efforts and see what God would do. I can say without doubt that He has never failed me, and He has often surprised me by doing something exceedingly better than I could even imagine.

For the past two days I have been dealing with worry about a situation, even though I know it does no good. Two times I heard God whisper in my heart that He would take care of it, but I still struggled to stop worrying. As of this morning, the situation is taken care of, and, I might add, it was done quite easily. The problem wasn't nearly as big as I had imagined, and once again I saw the faithfulness of God.

God is faithful, and He cannot lie. Therefore, we can trust the promises that are found in His Word, which number more than five thousand. He is a God of justice, which means He will always make right anything that is wrong in our lives. He brings our recompense and pays us back for any unjust treatment we have had in the past if we will trust Him to do so.

> For I, the Lord, love justice; I hate robbery and wrongdoing.
> In my faithfulness I will reward my people and make an
> everlasting covenant with them.
>
> Isaiah 61:8

God's Word teaches us that if we will humble ourselves under the mighty hand of God, He will lift us up in due time (1 Pet. 5:6). To humble ourselves means to be low-lying and to stay under. But our flesh doesn't want to stay under anything; it prefers to be over everything and in charge of everything.

Jesus told His disciples that the greatest among them "should be like the youngest, and the one who rules like the one who serves" (Luke 22:26). In other words, those who are truly great will stay under the mighty hand of God and resist walking in their own will. They won't push themselves forward but will wait for God to promote them. They won't try to make sure they are never taken advantage of, because they trust God to protect and care for them.

When our attitude is "I'm afraid that if I trust, I will get hurt," we live in misery. We become worn-out from always trying to stay in the number one position—the lead, on top, ahead, first, in charge, giving the orders, competing with anyone who might get ahead of us, and comparing ourselves and our positions in life with everyone else's. When we do these things, we are trying to do in our own strength something only God can do, and until we humble ourselves and realize that, we will continue to struggle.

How does this work in practical everyday life situations? Let's say I am playing golf with Dave, and he isn't playing very well. He gets grouchy with me because he is frustrated with his golf game. What should my response be? I can (and often do) lash out at him. I think, *You are not going to treat me like that and just get away with it.* My old nature thinks: *If I don't say or do something, this treatment may continue. And I'm going to make sure it doesn't.* Or, I can pray for Dave and trust God to deal with the situation. Which of these two options sounds the most peaceful?

There are times when confronting a person who is being rude or unkind to you is the right course of action, but there are also times when we should show mercy to those who offend us, remembering all the times we have not been on our best behavior, either. If we will allow ourselves to be guided by God's Spirit in these types of situations, we will always do the right thing.

Often when Jesus was accused of something wicked, He didn't even answer His accusers. He knew that God would deal with them in His own way and time. He was secure in His Father's love and had no need to defend Himself because He knew that God would defend Him.

Follow Jesus

Disciples of Christ are to discipline themselves to follow in His footsteps and handle situations as He did. We can see that the apostle Paul did this, and we should, too. Some of the people he went to help mistreated him. He wrote:

> Alexander the metalworker did me a great deal of harm. The Lord will repay him for what he has done. You too should be on your guard against him, because he strongly opposed our message. At my first defense, no one came to my support, but everyone deserted me. May it not be held against them. But the Lord stood at my side and gave me strength.
>
> 2 Timothy 4:14–17

Paul sacrificed and suffered greatly in order to help people, so we can just imagine how it hurt him when they did not stand by him in his hour of need. Please notice that Paul's response to the situation was to forgive them, and the result was that the Lord came and stood by him. I would rather have God stand by me than people, wouldn't you?

When we do things God's way rather than our own way, we always end up enjoying God's best for our lives, and that includes freedom from being afraid someone will take advantage of us. People who are afraid of being taken advantage of cannot wait on God for vindication when they are mistreated. They get emotional and begin functioning out of old wounds and fears rather than humbling themselves and waiting on Him.

> *People who are afraid of being taken advantage of cannot wait on God for vindication when they are mistreated.*

Trusting People

We can safely trust God fully in any situation, but we need to be more cautious when it comes to trusting people. We can trust people and should not allow suspicion to fill our minds, but because all people have weaknesses, we cannot trust them completely. We should be aware that people are imperfect and are likely to hurt us at times. If we have unrealistic expectations of others, we set ourselves up to be let down and disappointed.

Intimacy and close relationships can be maintained, but we should also use wisdom as we deal with other people. There are things we probably should not entrust to anyone except God. Personally, I don't mistrust anyone unless they have given me good reason to, but neither do I trust any human being the way I trust God. Jesus didn't mistrust His disciples, but He "did not entrust Himself to them," because He understood human nature and knew how people can be (John 2:24 AMP). Our total trust should be reserved for God alone, but we can definitely have close, intimate relationships with people. In fact, we need this type of connectedness with family and friends to fully enjoy life.

I encourage you not to isolate yourself for fear of being hurt or taken advantage of. Develop an intimate relationship with God and close relationships with other people, and if you need to, "do it afraid." If one relationship doesn't work out, don't assume others will be the same way. God has people set aside especially for you to be good friends with, so pray and ask for His guidance. Don't let fear make you afraid to trust!

Do not be afraid to give up the good to go for the great.

John D. Rockefeller

The Slingshot

When I was young—eight or nine years old—I had a strong fear of heights. I was getting to the age at which I was tall enough to ride roller coasters, and I distinctly remember my dad taking my siblings and me to Florida one year for a vacation. He packed us up in the car and drove us into the city, where we were presented with the giant steel death trap known as the Slingshot.

The hulking structure towered over me, two large pillars attached by elastic cables to a small, steel-framed sphere that seated two. I remember feeling small while staring up at it—smaller still when the mingling shouts of terror and joy floated down as the Slingshot's passengers were propelled upward.

I was ready to leave, but the grin on my dad's face revealed that he had a different idea. Guess whose turn was next? Yep.

I made every excuse I could, anything to avoid facing my fear. What's worse than falling from the sky? I'll tell you: being *shot up* into the sky first. Finally, my dad said, "It's your choice, but make sure you don't have regrets later from missing out on something fun."

A couple of minutes later, I was strapped into the ride's tiny cockpit. I gripped the handlebars so tightly that my knuckles turned white. The next thirty seconds blurred past: a sharp snap of the release mechanism; a heavy force pressing down on me as we pushed our way up and up and up; my dad laughing hysterically while I clung for dear life. And then it was done.

I felt lighter when I touched the ground—exhilarated, even. I was proud. My fear hadn't disappeared entirely, but I'd managed to overcome it. I trusted my dad when I was afraid, and he did not let me down. As a result, I was rewarded with a joyful memory and personal growth. We rode the Slingshot three more times that day.

Now, I think of that story whenever hard times come around. When I feel doubt or fear, I try my best to choose faith—not in my earthly dad, but in my heavenly Father. And I may not always know the result when the fear and uncertainty blur past, but I know that I can look back when my feet touch the ground and see His faithfulness all along the way.

—Shiloh

CHAPTER 23

You Can Rest in the Promise of Eternity

Freedom from the Fear of Death

And also that He might deliver and completely set free all those who through the [haunting] fear of death were held in bondage throughout the whole course of their lives.

Hebrews 2:15 AMPC

The word *death* is defined in *Vine's Complete Expository Dictionary* as "the separation of the soul (the spiritual part of man) from the body (the material part), the latter ceasing to function and turning to dust." If we were to look up *death* in most dictionaries, we would find the meaning to be something about ceasing to exist, but as we see from *Vine's Complete Expository Dictionary*, the biblical meaning of death doesn't say that we cease to exist, but that our bodies cease to function. The body does cease to exist, but the soul remains. Our soul is our inner life and it consists of our emotions, desires, thoughts, imaginings, and will. We might say it is the real us! So *we* don't cease to exist when we die; only our bodies do.

Believers have God's promise that we will be given new, glorified bodies after our earthly lives have ended. We will go to heaven to be with Him for all eternity! Being in heaven sounds like it will be wonderful:

> "He will wipe away every tear from their eyes. There will be no more death" or mourning or crying or pain, for the old order of things has passed away.
>
> Revelation 21:4

No one can function in the earthly realm without a flesh-and-bones body. That is why God sent His Son to help us and deliver us from the fear of death by dying in our place and paying for our sin. In order to do that, He had to have a physical body. He has experienced everything we do as humans because He had a human body, but He was fully God within that body. Jesus' dying for us doesn't mean that our bodies won't die, but it does mean we don't need to fear death because we know what will happen to us the moment we pass from this life: We will see God face-to-face. For those who have accepted Jesus as their Savior and Lord, the joy of living in His actual presence will be too marvelous to grasp until we experience it.

> We know what will happen to us the moment we pass from this life: We will see God face-to-face.

None of us wants to die before our time, but death does not need to frighten us. It simply means that we leave our temporary home on earth to go to our eternal home in heaven. We should always keep in mind that life here is temporary; this world really is not our home. That is one reason we never feel 100 percent satisfied. There is a longing in us to live in God's presence in an atmosphere of complete peace and love. Eternity is written in our hearts (Eccles. 3:11). Even those who do not believe in God have this same longing; they just don't know what it is. That's why they try to fill it with things, money, success, and other resources. Even Christians tend to do this, at least for a while, until they realize that they really don't want another thing; they want more of Jesus.

It is not wrong to want to enjoy the good things our earthly lives offer, but we should never let any of it come before God. *Keep God in first place at all times, and you will end up in the right place when you die.*

Because every person, without exception, will die one day, it is unwise to spend your life fearing something you cannot avoid. I would think that anyone who knows they are going to heaven would not wrestle with the fear of death, but many do.

The Apostle Paul Talked about Death

Paul wrote, "For to me, to live is Christ and to die is gain" (Phil. 1:21). He was ready to die anytime the Lord wanted to take him, but he also wanted to keep helping people. He said that he was "hard-pressed" between the two choices (Phil. 1:23 NKJV). His desire was to depart and be with Christ, because that would have been better. But he also realized that to remain in the flesh was more necessary for the people to whom he ministered (Phil. 1:23–24). It sure doesn't sound like Paul was afraid to die.

I find that the older I get, the more I look forward to being out of this world and all of its miseries and being with the Lord. But, like Paul, I want to stay on earth as long as God wants me to and finish the course He has put before me. I want to complete my race here, but I am not afraid of death.

When Paul wrote to the Corinthians about death and resurrection, he explained to them that even when a seed is sown in the ground, it dies or ceases to exist as a seed, and then it is resurrected or comes out of the ground as something entirely different (1 Cor. 15:36–38). I don't know about you, but I am excited to see what my glorified body will be like. I don't think it will have cellulite or need to be concerned about calories, and it won't be tired or get the flu or need a hip replacement!

What about Hell?

We would rather not think about hell, and if you have received Jesus by faith as your Savior and Lord, then you need not think about it except to be very glad you are not going there. But nonbelievers should be concerned.

Many people don't think that hell exists because they don't believe that a God of love would condemn anyone to such a horrible place. The truth is that God doesn't send anyone there. People have chosen to go there by the way they have lived their lives.

Yes, God is love, but He is also just. Sin requires a sacrifice to remediate sin, and Jesus came and sacrificed Himself for our sins (Isa. 53:5–12; Eph. 5:2; 1 John 4:10). He paid the debt we owed. He took our place and suffered on our behalf. Jesus did this for everyone who would ever live, but in order to receive His gift, we must believe in Him and what He did for us. God is not willing for anyone to perish (2 Pet. 3:9), but those who refuse to believe in Him have, in effect, condemned themselves to hell.

I know this is an uncomfortable subject. I find that I am uncomfortable even writing about it, but we must be aware of the possibility of hell's existence. I once read that there are sixty verses about hell in the four gospels, and all were the words of Jesus.

Speaking of hell, Jesus said, "There will be weeping there, and gnashing of teeth" (Luke 13:28). That sounds like extreme misery. We know what weeping is, but what is gnashing of teeth?

It means grinding the teeth together while holding the jaw very tight. We do that even now when we experience great pain. Other descriptions of hell in the Bible state that it will be filled with fire (Matt. 25:41; Mark 9:43; Jude 7). It also says that unrepentant sinners will be cast into the lake that burns with fire (Rev. 20:15).

One of Jesus' parables makes it quite clear that both heaven and hell exist and that those in hell can see into heaven (Luke 16:19–31). The parable tells of a rich man who was clothed in the finest cloth and feasted sumptuously every day. At his gate, some people had left a poor man named Lazarus, who was covered with sores and desired to be fed with what fell from the rich man's table. Moreover, even the dogs came and licked his sores. The poor man died, and angels carried him to Abraham's side. The rich man also died and was buried. In Hades (hell) and in torment, the rich man lifted up his eyes and saw Abraham afar off and Lazarus at his side. And he called out, "Father Abraham, have pity and mercy on me and send Lazarus to dip the tip of his finger in water and cool my tongue, for I am in anguish in this flame" (Luke 16:24 AMPC).

We know from this parable that the man in hell could see those in heaven. I would think being in hell and having to look at what we missed would be torture. The rich man enjoyed himself on earth with no concern for others who were hurting, and now he was experiencing the punishment he deserved. The poor man, on the other hand, was receiving his reward in heaven.

We can see that heaven and hell both exist. Hell is a place we don't want to go, so it is important to make the right decisions while we can.

> *Heaven and hell both exist. Hell is a place we don't want to go, so it is important to make the right decisions while we can.*

Resurrection

Jesus died in our place and took our punishment for sin, but thankfully the story doesn't end with His death. On the third day after His death and burial, He was resurrected (Luke 24). Death could not hold Him down, and it cannot hold us down if we believe in Jesus. Death had no power over Him, and it has no power over us except the power we give it by fearing it while we are alive.

Muslims believe in the teachings of a prophet named Muhammad, who is dead. Buddhists believe in the teachings of a man named Siddhārtha Gautama, also known as the Buddha, who is also dead. Many other religions base their faith on someone who is dead, but Christians believe in Jesus, who is alive!

Believers need no proof of the resurrection, because the proof is in our hearts. But for those who don't believe, it may be helpful to know that proof of the resurrection does exist. We have numerous resurrection accounts from Christ's disciples and Roman soldiers who guarded the tomb. They witnessed the empty tomb with the grave clothes left behind and the burial napkin that covered his face neatly folded and left to the side (John 20:6–7).

Is there any particular significance to the napkin being folded? I recently read an article that presented a beautiful truth about that. Jesus used many parables and cultural references to get His messages across. In His day, a servant prepared meals for their master and would not dare to touch the table until the master finished eating. If the master ate, took his napkin, wiped his hands and beard, wadded the napkin up, and then placed it on the table, that meant he was finished and everything could be cleaned up. However, if he folded his napkin, no servant would touch the table because the folded napkin meant "I am coming back!"

Was Jesus leaving us a message with the folded napkin? I think He was. I think everything Jesus did had a purpose and the folded napkin had one also. Jesus promised that He will come back for us, so we know that death will not have the final word.

> Do not let your hearts be troubled. You believe in God; believe also in me. My Father's house has many rooms; if that were not so, would I have told you that I am going there to prepare a place for you? And if I go and prepare a place for you, I will come back and take you to be with me that you also may be where I am.
>
> John 14:1–3

Many people spend their lives terrified of death. William Randolph Hearst was an extremely wealthy man who built and lived in a mansion filled with lovely things. When anyone visited, he had a strict rule: No one was allowed to talk about or even mention death. He was tormented each night as he went to bed that he might die during the night. Interestingly enough, Hearst's fear of death didn't prevent him from dying. It only ruined his enjoyment of living.

On the other hand, we have the testimony of many others, such as the apostle Paul, who were ready to leave this earth anytime. The early church father John Chrysostom had a zeal for reform in the church and infuriated Empress Eudoxia, who exiled him many times. He said, "What can I fear? Will it be death? But you know that Christ is my life, and that I shall gain by death."

Let us look forward to heaven rather than fearing death, for when we leave this earth, our life is just beginning.

When we leave this earth, our life is just beginning.

Are We Afraid of Death—or of Dying?

In thinking about the time of my death, I can honestly say that I do not fear death at all, but I do hope that dying is not very painful. Once I was on a small airplane with one other person. Suddenly, with no explanation from the pilots, the plane began to descend very rapidly, and we thought it would probably crash. We held hands and prepared to meet Jesus, but I will admit the one thought I had was, "I wonder if this will hurt very much."

I think most of us pray that when our time comes, we will go to sleep and just wake up in heaven, or that God will take us quickly with no lingering illness. Why not pray for the best? However, we must also know that whatever the process of dying entails for each of us, God will be with us and usher us home at exactly the right moment.

I have heard many stories of people on their deathbeds saying, "Jesus is here for me now. I have to go." Dying is something no one can avoid. We may feel some fear of the unknown, but we have assurance of the resurrection and heaven, and that is cause to celebrate!

It takes courage to grow up and become who you really are.
E. E. Cummings

Everyone deals with fear, but we can learn not to let it dictate our decisions or rule our lives. I doubt that fear will ever completely disappear from anyone's life, but we can and should resist it. If you need to do something afraid in order to do it, gather all your courage and take a step of faith. I certainly would not be doing the things I am doing today had I not stepped out when I believed God wanted me to, even when fear was screaming at me, "You're going to fail!" As the old saying goes, "If at first you don't succeed, try, try again." But I say, if at first you don't succeed, *you are normal!* Keep trying until you find your sweet spot in life.

I want to close this book by encouraging you to not let the fear of being different steal your destiny. In order to be who you really are, you must realize that you never will be just like anyone else, nor can you be. You are unique, and that is what makes you special. Ralph Waldo Emerson wrote, "Whoso would be a man, must be a nonconformist." It's so important not to spend our time and energy trying to be like other people.

People want to be free to be individuals, yet they fear being different. Why? Because in the past they have been rejected because they didn't fit into someone else's idea of what they should be or do.

Human nature causes people to fear the pain of rejection, so we conform. Most people find there is safety in conformity. Jesus, the apostle Paul, and everyone else who ever accomplished anything great were nonconformists. We are to be transformed into Christ's image, but we must never conform to the world (2 Cor. 3:18; Rom. 12:2).

I tend to think that if we can successfully confront the fear of being different and become who we truly are, we will be able to conquer any other fear that comes against us.

I pray this book has helped you and will continue to do so. Live life bravely and enjoy all of it!

EMPOWERING SCRIPTURES TO HELP YOU FIGHT FEAR

Nothing will help you fight the temptation to fear and to do things afraid like the power of God's Word. I encourage you to read, meditate on, and even memorize these scriptures so you can call them to mind readily whenever fear begins to arise in your heart.

> There is no fear in love; but perfect love casts out fear, because fear involves torment. But he who fears has not been made perfect in love.
>
> 1 John 4:18 NKJV

> God gave us a spirit not of fear but of power and love and self-control.
>
> 2 Timothy 1:7 ESV

> Have I not commanded you? Be strong and courageous. Do not be afraid; do not be discouraged, for the Lord your God will be with you wherever you go.
>
> Joshua 1:9

> So do not fear, for I am with you; do not be dismayed, for I am your God. I will strengthen you and help you; I will uphold you with my righteous right hand.
>
> Isaiah 41:10

But now, this is what the Lord says—he who created you, Jacob, he who formed you, Israel: "Do not fear, for I have redeemed you; I have summoned you by name; you are mine."

Isaiah 43:1

For I am convinced that neither death nor life, neither angels nor demons, neither the present nor the future, nor any powers, neither height nor depth, nor anything else in all creation, will be able to separate us from the love of God that is in Christ Jesus our Lord.

Romans 8:38–39

The Lord is with me; I will not be afraid. What can mere mortals do to me?

Psalm 118:6

Peace I leave with you; my peace I give you. I do not give to you as the world gives. Do not let your hearts be troubled and do not be afraid.

John 14:27

When I am afraid, I put my trust in you.

Psalm 56:3

"The Lord himself goes before you and will be with you; he will never leave you nor forsake you. Do not be afraid; do not be discouraged."

Deuteronomy 31:8

You will keep in perfect peace those whose minds are steadfast, because they trust in you.

Isaiah 26:3

Cast all your anxiety on him because he cares for you.

1 Peter 5:7

The Lord is my light and my salvation—whom shall I fear? The Lord is the stronghold of my life—of whom shall I be afraid?

Psalm 27:1

Even though I walk through the darkest valley, I will fear no evil, for you are with me; your rod and your staff, they comfort me.

Psalm 23:4

Therefore do not worry about tomorrow, for tomorrow will worry about itself. Each day has enough trouble of its own.

Matthew 6:34

"For I know the plans I have for you," declares the Lord, "plans to prosper you and not to harm you, plans to give you hope and a future."

Jeremiah 29:11

Do you have a real relationship with Jesus?

God loves you! He created you to be a special, unique, one-of-a-kind individual, and He has a specific purpose and plan for your life. And through a personal relationship with your Creator—God—you can discover a way of life that will truly satisfy your soul.

No matter who you are, what you've done, or where you are in your life right now, God's love and grace are greater than your sin—your mistakes. Jesus willingly gave His life so you can receive forgiveness from God and have new life in Him. He's just waiting for you to invite Him to be your Savior and Lord.

If you are ready to commit your life to Jesus and follow Him, all you have to do is ask Him to forgive your sins and give you a fresh start in the life you are meant to live. Begin by praying this prayer...

> *Lord Jesus, thank You for giving Your life for me and forgiving me of my sins so I can have a personal relationship with You. I am sincerely sorry for the mistakes I've made, and I know I need You to help me live right.*
>
> *Your Word says in Romans 10:9, "If you declare with your mouth, 'Jesus is Lord,' and believe in your heart that God raised him from the dead, you will be saved" (NIV). I believe You are the Son of God and confess You as my Savior and Lord. Take me just as I am, and work in my heart, making me the person You want me to be. I want to live for You, Jesus, and I am so grateful that You are giving me a fresh start in my new life with You today.*
>
> *I love You, Jesus!*

It's so amazing to know that God loves us so much! He wants to have a deep, intimate relationship with us that grows every day as we spend time with Him in prayer and Bible study. And we want to encourage you in your new life in Christ.

Please visit joycemeyer.org/salvation to request Joyce's book *A New Way of Living*, which is our gift to you. We also have other free resources online to help you make progress in pursuing everything God has for you.

Congratulations on your fresh start in your life in Christ! We hope to hear from you soon.

JOYCE MEYER is one of the world's leading practical Bible teachers. A *New York Times* bestselling author, Joyce's books have helped millions of people find hope and restoration through Jesus Christ. Joyce's programs, *Enjoying Everyday Life* and *Everyday Answers with Joyce Meyer*, air around the world on television, radio, and the Internet. Through Joyce Meyer Ministries, Joyce teaches internationally on a number of topics with a particular focus on how the Word of God applies to our everyday lives. Her candid communication style allows her to share openly and practically about her experiences so others can apply what she has learned to their lives.

Joyce has authored more than one hundred books, which have been translated into more than one hundred languages, and over 65 million of her books have been distributed worldwide. Bestsellers include *Power Thoughts*; *The Confident Woman*; *Look Great, Feel Great*; *Starting Your Day Right*; *Ending Your Day Right*; *Approval Addiction*; *How to Hear from God*; *Beauty for Ashes*; and *Battlefield of the Mind*.

Joyce's passion to help hurting people is foundational to the vision of Hand of Hope, the missions arm of Joyce Meyer Ministries. Hand of Hope provides worldwide humanitarian outreach such as feeding programs, medical care, orphanages, disaster response, human trafficking intervention and rehabilitation, and much more—always sharing the love and gospel of Christ.

U.S. & FOREIGN OFFICE
ADDRESSES

Joyce Meyer Ministries
P.O. Box 655
Fenton, MO 63026
USA
(636) 349-0303

Joyce Meyer Ministries—Canada
P.O. Box 7700
Vancouver, BC V6B 4E2
Canada
(800) 868-1002

Joyce Meyer Ministries—Australia
Locked Bag 77
Mansfield Delivery Centre
Queensland 4122
Australia
(07) 3349 1200

Joyce Meyer Ministries—England
P.O. Box 1549
Windsor SL4 1GT
United Kingdom
01753 831102

Joyce Meyer Ministries—South Africa
P.O. Box 5
Cape Town 8000
South Africa
(27) 21-701-1056

100 Inspirational Quotes
100 Ways to Simplify Your Life
21 Ways to Finding Peace and Happiness
Any Minute
Approval Addiction
The Approval Fix
The Battle Belongs to the Lord
*Battlefield of the Mind**
Battlefield of the Mind Bible
Battlefield of the Mind for Kids
Battlefield of the Mind for Teens
Battlefield of the Mind Devotional
Battlefield of the Mind New Testament
*Be Anxious for Nothing**
Beauty for Ashes
Being the Person God Made You to Be
Change Your Words, Change Your Life
Colossians: A Biblical Study
The Confident Mom
The Confident Woman
The Confident Woman Devotional
Do Yourself a Favor . . . Forgive
Eat the Cookie . . . Buy the Shoes
Eight Ways to Keep the Devil under Your Feet
Ending Your Day Right
Enjoying Where You Are on the Way to Where You Are Going
Ephesians: A Biblical Study
The Everyday Life Bible
The Everyday Life Psalms and Proverbs
Filled with the Spirit
Galatians: A Biblical Study
Good Health, Good Life
Habits of a Godly Woman
*Healing the Soul of a Woman**
Healing the Soul of a Woman Devotional
Hearing from God Each Morning
*How to Hear from God**
How to Succeed at Being Yourself
I Dare You
*If Not for the Grace of God**
In Pursuit of Peace
James: A Biblical Study
The Joy of Believing Prayer
Knowing God Intimately
A Leader in the Making
Life in the Word

Living beyond Your Feelings
Living Courageously
Look Great, Feel Great
Love Out Loud
The Love Revolution
Making Good Habits, Breaking Bad Habits
Making Marriage Work (previously published as Help Me—I'm Married!)
Me and My Big Mouth!*
The Mind Connection*
Never Give Up!
Never Lose Heart
New Day, New You
Overload
The Penny
Perfect Love (previously published as God Is Not Mad at You)*
The Power of Being Positive
The Power of Being Thankful
The Power of Determination
The Power of Forgiveness
The Power of Simple Prayer
Power Thoughts
Power Thoughts Devotional
Reduce Me to Love
The Secret Power of Speaking God's Word
The Secret to True Happiness
The Secrets of Spiritual Power
Seven Things That Steal Your Joy
Start Your New Life Today
Starting Your Day Right
Straight Talk
Teenagers Are People Too!
Trusting God Day by Day
Woman to Woman
The Word, the Name, the Blood
You Can Begin Again
Your Battles Belong to the Lord*

JOYCE MEYER SPANISH TITLES

Belleza en Lugar de Cenizas (Beauty for Ashes)
Buena Salud, Buena Vida (Good Health, Good Life)
Cambia Tus Palabras, Cambia Tu Vida (Change Your Words, Change Your Life)
El Campo de Batalla de la Mente (Battlefield of the Mind)
Como Formar Buenos Habitos y Romper Malos Habitos (Making Good Habits,
Breaking Bad Habits)
La Conexión de la Mente (The Mind Connection)
Dios No Está Enojado Contigo (God Is Not Mad at You)
La Dosis de Aprobación (The Approval Fix)

Efesios: Comentario Biblico (Ephesians: Biblical Commentary)
Empezando Tu Día Bien (Starting Your Day Right)
Hazte un Favor a Ti Mismo... Perdona (Do Yourself a Favor... Forgive)
Madre Segura de Sí Misma (The Confident Mom)
Pensamientos de Poder (Power Thoughts)
Sanidad para el Alma de una Mujer (Healing the Soul of a Woman)
Santiago: Comentario Bíblico (James: Biblical Commentary)
Sobrecarga (Overload)*
Sus Batallas Son del Señor (Your Battles Belong to the Lord)
Termina Bien tu Día (Ending Your Day Right)
Usted Puede Comenzar de Nuevo (You Can Begin Again)
Viva Valientemente (Living Courageously)

*Study Guide available for this title

BOOKS BY DAVE MEYER

Life Lines